CRITICAL
INFORMATION LITERACY

CRITICAL
INFORMATION LITERACY

FOUNDATIONS, INSPIRATION, AND IDEAS

Annie Downey

Library Juice Press
Sacramento, CA

Published by Library Juice Press in 2016

Library Juice Press
PO Box 188784
Sacramento CA 95818

http://libraryjuicepress.com

This book is printed on acid-free, sustainably-sourced paper

Library of Congress Cataloging-in-Publication Data

Names: Downey, Annie, 1974- author.
Title: Critical information literacy : foundations, inspiration, and ideas /
    by Annie Downey.
Description: Sacramento, CA : Library Juice Press, 2016. | Includes
    bibliographical references and index.
Identifiers: LCCN 2016017128 | ISBN 9781634000246 (alk. paper)
Subjects: LCSH: Information literacy. | Information literacy--Study and
    teaching (Higher) | Academic libraries--Relations with faculty and
    curriculum. | Academic librarians--Professional relationships. | Critical
    pedagogy. | Transformative learning.
Classification: LCC ZA3075 .D69 2016 | DDC 028.7--dc23
LC record available at https://lccn.loc.gov/2016017128

TABLE OF CONTENTS

To Mike

ACKNOWLEDGEMENTS

As with any book project, this one was supported by many people who deserve more from me than this little section of text can provide. First, thanks to my brilliant and kind dissertation advisor, Dr. Amy Fann, who provided me with continuous and thoughtful guidance and expert support and never lost faith that I would finish, even as I had a baby and moved across the country. Thanks also to my dissertation committee members, Dr. Yunfei Du and Dr. Beverly Bower. This book is the direct result of my work with many smart, insightful, and dedicated librarians, including those I interviewed for my study and many wonderful colleagues at UNT and Reed, including but not limited to (and in no particular order): Jo Monahan, Lilly Ramin, Starr Hoffman, Julie Leuzinger, Cindy Batman, Suzanne Sears, Gayla Byerly, Rebecca Barham, Linda Maddux, Dena Hutto, Joe Marquez, Angie Beiriger, and Erin Conor.

Thank you to my dear mother, Margie Jones-Keefer, for showing me the importance and value of hard work and never giving up. Thanks to my sister, Kendra Keefer-McGee, for introducing me to Paulo Freire and encouraging me to work for a more just world; and my brothers, Andrew and Jesse Keefer, for letting me know all the time that they believe in and are proud of their big sister. My intelligent, funny, and curious children, Maggie Anne, Livvie, and Sophie, inspire me and keep me going every day. And finally, thank you to Mike who took care of the house, the kids, and me unfailingly throughout both the dissertation process and the crazy year I decided to publish two books – all while providing constant love and encouragement.

Introduction

What Does Critical Information Literacy Do?

By Jessica Critten

When we talk about critical information literacy, we often discuss its relationship to information literacy, or how critical information literacy changes our practice. Certainly we talk about the importance of information and knowledge for liberation and empowerment. However, we don't often talk about how critical information literacy conceives of "information" itself. Just focusing on the word 'information' in the term 'Critical Information Literacy' (CIL) could even redefine the whole concept: do we work to realize an information literacy that is critical, or are we aiming for a level of deftness with critical information? I don't mean to get overly semantic here as to miss the point of the whole endeavor. Rather, I wonder at the possibilities of "critical information": does it change our definitions? Does it change how we create, use, and learn about information?

Buckland (1991) famously proposed that information can have materiality as a "thing" that informs (and therefore, I would add, something that can be commodified), but can also be a communication process or an epistemology: information is the process of knowing, and knowledge itself.[1] There are any number of similar analyses of the term "information" but I mention this one for the way that it signals the socio-cultural (and also personal) contextuality of information. In other words, certain things, processes, or knowledge mean different things to different people in different situations. It seems to suggest that information is a living, changing, subjective idea. Information

---

1   Michael Buckland, "Information as Thing," *Journal of The American Society for Information Science*, 42, no.5 (1991): 351-360.

here is a *language,* or, at least, is brought to life by a language that allows it to be understood and communicated. I would locate this concept of 'critical information' in the site where information, language, and meaning become interconnected. Critical information is not just the message itself, but also the context in which it is transmitted and understood. It recognizes its socially constructed nature and the political and cultural implications that come with it.

If this is what critical information is, then I am next struck with the question, what does it *do?* How does it function? What might it change, if we've gone to the trouble of defining it as a thing separate from "information" itself? As Downey explores throughout this book, critical information literacy gives us a context and an energy that makes it a productive space to explore these questions. So to that end, I rephrase slightly and ask, what does critical information literacy do? Karen Nicholson outlines "two broad goals" of critical information literacy: "...the first is to bridge the gap that separates practice from theory within librarianship and the broader LIS discipline...[and] to bring in outside approaches and disciplinary perspectives to bear on IL."[2] I'll use these goals as guideposts below.

What Does Critical Information Literacy Do for Our Research?

One of the most salient themes of this book is that conversations (and controversies) about CIL almost always include the perceived tension between theory and practice. That is, there is a sense that theory is impractical and practice is atheoretical. This is a false dichotomy that has in many situations halted the progress and adoption of critical information literacy throughout the profession. I would offer that perhaps this tension often comes from a deeper disagreement or misunderstanding about the field of librarianship itself: what kind of "science" "library science" actually is. Are we like a natural science, beholden to positivist scientific methods that might allow us to predict user behavior? Or are we a social science that recognizes the fundamental complexity (and, perhaps, unknowability) of human beings and aims not to *predict,* but rather to *understand* human

---

2   Karen P. Nicholson, "Information Literacy as a Situated Practice in the Neoliberal University," *Proceedings of the Annual Conference of CAIS* (2014): 2.

phenomena. Choosing a "science" here informs what our scholarship looks like (and therefore what our evidence looks like.) We have to choose. We cannot be both.

If we are like a natural science, information literacy is a cognitive process that can be taught as a series of discrete and observable skills because we assert that human behavior follows a logical and rational pattern. Therefore, we can assess effectiveness and value using a matrix of standards. If we are a social science, we are moved to confront the idea that perhaps our efforts are not so easily measured as human behavior is itself not so easily measured. Moreover, the matrix we are concerned with is not one of standards but of a complex interplay of human affect, politics, and culture. If we are a natural science, we might concern ourselves primarily with practice as the observable domain of our work, the site where we can determine with certainty and objectivity that our efforts are productive. Theory in this space is more than likely the work of cognitivism and behaviorism, and is conceived of as a roadmap towards some kind of achievable truth. Theory and practice are inseparable because the latter is proof of the former.

If we are a social science, we might challenge the idea that evidence and proof are the same thing, or that proof is desirable (or achievable.) As such, we could consider practice as possible evidence of theory and theory as a spark towards understanding. Theory and practice might also be the same thing in this space, considering as philosopher H.G. Gadamer (1982) does that theory is a practical philosophy; that is, that having some theoretical basis to inform our thought processes and behaviors is itself practical.[3] In other words, theory is practical because theory helps us make decisions.

One of the most remarkable things critical information literacy does for our research, then, is to very clearly assert that information literacy and the work of librarianship is a **social science.** Specifically, it is what Lather (2006) describes as "less comfortable" social science "...full of stuck places and difficult philosophical issues of truth, interpretation and responsibility."[4] As such, CIL is more than just

---

3   H. G. Gadamer, "Hermeneutics as a Practical Philosophy," *Reason in the Age of Science.* (Cambridge, MA: MIT Press, 1982).

4   Patti Lather, "Paradigm Proliferation as a Good Thing to Think With: Teaching Research in Education as a Wild Profusion," *International Journal of Qualitative Studies in Education* 19 (2006): 52.

a philosophy of information literacy and research (or information literacy with a critical hat) it seems to me to actually be a criticism of the work of traditional information literacy itself. Information literacy emerged as a way to make an abstract, tacit, and complex process more concrete,[5] and wrongly cast the work of research as a discrete and skills-based process. Traditional skills-based informational literacy as realized in the ACRL Information Literacy Standards (as opposed to critical information literacy) is a manifestation of the conception of librarianship and information literacy as a natural science. Downey further explores the implications and legacy of these standards within the field of information literacy in chapter 1.

What Does Critical Information Literacy Do in Our Learning Spaces?

As Downey notes in chapter 3, the librarians she interviewed for her research study overwhelmingly expressed their disappointment with the scarcity of opportunities to learn about and practice critical approaches to teaching. If librarians are taught anything at all about instruction in library school it is often actually about instructional design; that is, how do we craft a learning outcome? How do we include moments for active learning? How might we scaffold content so that each new idea builds on the preceding one? This focus on curriculum planning and teaching methods continues in the content of most library instruction conferences, where practitioners more often than not discuss pedagogy, even if they don't specifically characterize it that way (examples include sessions that highlight techniques for engaging students with examples from popular culture, or describing the differences between popular and scholarly sources as a wrestling match.) I am not aiming to discount necessary and thoughtful discussions of pedagogy as a whole. Rather, I aim to question the dominance of these kinds of demonstrations in spaces dedicated to educational and professional discourse.

Critical information literacy requires that in addition to talking about *how* we teach we talk about *what* we teach. It does rightfully focus

---

5   Robert Farrell. "Reconsidering the Relationship between Generic and Situated IL Approaches: The Dreyfus Model of Skill Acquisition in Formal Information Literacy Learning Environments, Part I." *Library Philosophy & Practice* (2012): 1-16.

on pedagogy—specifically (as Downey notes) by way of experiential education, critical pedagogy, and transformative learning—but those philosophical approaches also ask us, as Nicholson did above, to examine how the interdisciplinarity of information might shape the curriculum itself, what Downey calls "critical content" in chapter 5. CIL encourages (or, perhaps more accurately, *challenges)* library practitioners to reach outside of our immediate field of vision and incorporate scholarship and theory from different disciplines. Critical information literacy in particular is an amalgam of philosophy, education, political science, and anthropology (among other disciplines.) Incorporating this interdisciplinarity into the library instruction curriculum has been increasingly discussed as "situating" information literacy within subject disciplines.[6] More than just placing information into its disciplinary context, though, situating information literacy also works to turn students into "human capital" within the larger context of the knowledge economy (Nicholson, 2014).[7] All of which is to say, it's not enough to challenge the skills agenda of "traditional" information literacy by placing information into a larger disciplinary context if those disciplines might also function as mechanisms of control. When we present information literacy as a set of practices within a discourse community, we still may not be investigating how those practices became institutionalized. We are still not reflecting on *what* we teach, we are just reifying current practices in a more disciplinary context.

That said, critical information *has* to be "situated" if it is, as we understand it, fundamentally contextual. This requires that we conceive of a situated *critical* information literacy, differentiated from situated information literacy in its emphasis on the processes that institutionalize certain disciplinary discourses. Situated critical information literacy does not just consider the subject discipline,

---

6 See among others: Robert Farrell, and William Badke, "Situating Information Literacy in the Disciplines: A Practical and Systematic Approach for Academic Librarians," *Reference Services Review* 43, no.2 (2015): 319-340.; Vesa Kautto and Sanna Talja, "Disciplinary Socialization: Learning to Evaluate the Quality of Scholarly Literature," *Advances in Library Administration and Organization* 25 (2007): 3-59.; Nichols, James T., "The 3 Directions: Situated Information Literacy," *College & Research Libraries* 70, no. 6 (2009): 515-530.

7 Karen P. Nicholson, "Information Literacy as a Situated Practice in the Neoliberal University," *Proceedings of the Annual Conference of CAIS* (2014):1.

but also the way that information is situated within a system of power relationships. In other words, if situated information literacy asks, "What are the conceptual and material research practices of a discipline?" A situated critical information literacy might ask, "Why are these the material and conceptual shared practices of a discipline? Who do they benefit? What voices are absent?"

As Downey notes in Chapter 6, this approach requires a lot of critical librarians. It requires professional autonomy to create one's own curriculum. It requires the privilege of time and access to expand one's knowledge base. It requires emotional labor to engage in liberatory projects. It requires personal and administrative comfort in not receiving immediate, observable results. To pretend towards any kind of ease in this project would be disingenuous. Which is all to say, so much of what critical information literacy might do in a learning space depends upon context and privilege.

WHAT *WILL* CRITICAL INFORMATION LITERACY DO?

I struggled with structuring this introduction around a question that seems to suggest that critical information literacy should have an "outcome": what does critical information literacy *do*? This kind of language too often gets co-opted in neoliberal projects to demonstrate "value" and promote "skills": "What will you need to know in order to be able to 'do' something?" Making critical librarianship into a verb seems in this sense instinctively wrong if, as Downey (by way of Mezirow and transformative learning) notes in chapter 2, the "goal" or "outcome" of critical work is *emancipation* or *liberation* rather than *prediction*. And yet, despite all that, I kept the framing device. Because, regardless of how problematic it might be, it underscored that for all that critical information literacy might be theoretical, for all that it might be reflective, for all that it might be personal, it is also an action. It is a call for resistance and change. Critical information literacy is, as is information, what we know and also what we *do*. Despite the connotations attached to it because of its relationship to theory, it is not a space for navel-gazing. Nor is it just a pedagogy or something that can be manifested with a few tweaks to a lesson plan. It is the knowledge and the application of the knowledge. The theory *and* the practice.

So with that, what is the future of critical information literacy? Anyone who attempts to pontificate about the future of libraries is probably not to be trusted, so I won't try. What I will do is lay out what I hope the future looks like, given my understanding of what critical information literacy *does*.

Cushla Kaptizke (2003) describes information literacy as presenting itself as "apolitical" and "emphasiz[ing] the consumption of information but lack[ing] metaknowledge because it neglects the sociocultural, historical and ideological processes of knowledge construction and justification."[8] Because of this, I find "information literacy" problematic for its gesture towards neutrality. I hope that, as we move forward, we reckon with the implications of not doing critical information literacy; that is, is there a problem with presenting research concepts and mechanics as straightforward and objective processes? If we aren't critical, are we anti-critical? I'm not sure. Downey's discussion about the differences between critical information literacy and information literacy in chapter 8 might be a good place for this discussion to continue.

I hope that as (if?) critical information literacy and critical librarianship become more popular and eventually institutionalized that we take advantage of this popularity to be subversive.[9] That is, if critical librarianship becomes watered down or paid lip service as a trend on the upswing, let's use that opportunity to change our curriculum (that is, what we teach, not just how we teach) or to advocate for a stronger presence in library or school policy making. This is an opportunity to co-opt the system to say "no" to that same system. All that said, I do not mean to refer to the possibility of the widespread adoption of critical paradigms cynically. As much as institutionalization can become a site of subversion, it also provides opportunities for increased awareness and support. Downey very powerfully acknowledges the importance of critical communities not just for "getting things done," but also for helping critical workers articulate and cultivate their professional identities.

I hope that our scholarship challenges the "quantitative assessment culture" that Downey discusses in chapter 7. In positioning positivism,

---

8   Cushla Kapitzke, "Information Literacy: A Positivist Epistemology and a Politics of Outformation." *Educational Theory* 53, no. 1 (2003): 46-7.

9   See: Maura Seale. "Institutionalizing Critical Librarianship," (Paper presented at the Critical Librarianship and Pedagogy Symposium, Tucson, Arizona, February 26, 2016).

quantitative methods, scientism, and evidence-based practice as the dominant research paradigms in librarianship, research in LIS often oversimplifies complex human behaviors and relationships and actively devalues alternative epistemologies and ways of knowing. As April Hathcock (2016) notes in her blog post, "Decolonizing Social Justice Work," "We want to step away from the white, male, Western mainstream and gather intellectual work from the margins. We want to feel comfortable citing examples from Grandmama and Miss Peachy down the street, even as others cite wisdom from Althusser or Marx."[10] Critical information literacy should give weight to these perspectives and challenge how so many of the methodologies we reproduce in our own work and teach to our students reify colonialism and sexism.

In that same vein, let's work to complicate how "information literacy" has shaped its subject: the student. What would our research and learning spaces look like if we aimed to conceive of our students as David James Hudson did in his 2016 keynote for the Critical Librarianship and Pedagogy Symposium, as having "identities [that are] both unstable and constructed, and material and real"?[11]

Lastly, I hope that critical information literacy becomes a space that inspires and cultivates resistance. Resistance is the other side of the coin of critical projects; we can't just have a critical information literacy that identifies problems, we have to have a community that supports efforts to challenge the institutions that create those problems. This all begins with turning the lens back on librarianship to identify what exists in our structures that perpetuates librarian precarity. If we want to be critical, we have to support each other so that resistance is not a privilege for the few, but a right for all.

---

10   April Hathcock, "Decolonizing Social Justice Work," *At the Intersection*. March 2, 2016.
      https://aprilhathcock.wordpress.com/2016/03/02/decolonizing-social-justice-work/

11   David James Hudson, "On Critical Librarianship and Pedagogies of the Practical,"
      (Keynote presented at the Critical Librarianship and Pedagogy Symposium, Tucson,
      Arizona, February 25, 2016).

WORKS CITED

Buckland, Michael. "Information as Thing." *Journal of The American Society for Information Science* 42, no. 5 (1991): 351-360.

Farrell, Robert. "Reconsidering the Relationship Between Generic and Situated IL Approaches: The Dreyfus Model of Skill Acquisition in Formal Information Literacy Learning Environments, Part I." *Library Philosophy & Practice* (2012): 1-16.

Farrell, Robert, and Badke, William. "Situating Information Literacy in the Disciplines: A Practical and Systematic Approach for Academic Librarians." *Reference Services Review* 43, no.2 (2015): 319-340.

Gadamer, Hans Georg. "Hermeneutics as a Practical Philosophy." *Reason in the Age of Science.* Cambridge, MA: MIT Press, 1982

Hathcock, April. "Decolonizing Social Justice Work." *At the Intersection.* March 2, 2016. https://aprilhathcock.wordpress.com/2016/03/02/decolonizing-social-justice-work/

Hudson, David James. "On Critical Librarianship and Pedagogies of the Practical." Keynote presented at the Critical Librarianship and Pedagogy Symposium, Tucson, Arizona, February 25, 2016.

Kapitzke, Cushla. "Information Literacy: A Positivist Epistemology and a Politics of Outformation." *Educational Theory* 53, no. 1 (2003): 37-53.

Kautto, Vesa, and Sanna Talja. "Disciplinary Socialization: Learning to Evaluate the Quality of Scholarly Literature." *Advances in Library Administration and Organization* 25 (2007): 3-59.

Lather, Patti. "Paradigm Proliferation as a Good Thing to Think With: Teaching Research in Education as a Wild Profusion." *International Journal of Qualitative Studies in Education* 19 (2006): 35-57.

Nichols, James T. "The 3 Directions: Situated Information Literacy." *College & Research Libraries* 70, no. 6 (2009): 515-530.

Nicholson, Karen P. "Information Literacy as a Situated Practice in the Neoliberal University." *Proceedings of the Annual Conference of CAIS* (2014).

Seale, Maura. "Institutionalizing Critical Librarianship." Paper presented at the Critical Librarianship and Pedagogy Symposium, Tucson, Arizona, February 26, 2016.

Chapter 1

Creating Informed Citizens in the Network Society: Problematizing the Legacy of Standards-Based Information Literacy

John Dewey argued in *Democracy and Education*[1] that the primary goal of education is to produce functioning, well-rounded, reflective, and thoughtful citizens to further and enhance democracy. He posited that to reach this goal, education must be grounded in experience, useful and meaningful for students, and should help us move towards a socially just society. In short, social justice depends on informed and engaged citizens. In the not too distant past, it was fairly simple to be an informed citizen by watching the evening news and reading the daily newspapers and an occasional book or magazine. Newspapers, television, and radio were easy to use information formats that were limited in terms of the programming and content available. Most households had access to three major networks on television, a limited dial of available radio stations that could be reached via antenna, and one or two local newspapers along with some access to a major city newspaper like the *New York Times* or the *Wall Street Journal*.

In the current world, the amount of information available in the traditional formats is essentially limitless, causing noted information literacy scholar Ilene Rockman to argue over ten years ago that "the issue is no longer one of not having enough information; it is just the opposite—too much information, in various formats and not all of

---

1   Dewey, *Democracy and Education: An Introduction to the Philosophy of Education.*

equal value."[2] Meanwhile, other types of information sources have exploded to include blogs, news and content aggregators, homegrown video and radio, commercially created online content, online journals and newspapers, massive archives, constantly growing government documents and databases, enormous online ebook and other digital collections, and on and on.

Americans have adapted quickly to the change in information availability, consuming an average of almost twelve hours of information each day, which includes 100,500 words per person. The amount of words Americans read tripled from 1980 to 2008 due to the Internet. From 2008 to 2013, the percentage of adults using the Internet grew from 75% to 85%, with 98% of teens and young adults in the United States regularly using the Internet. In the same span of time the Internet grew in size from over 186 million to 634 million websites. Further, 85% of young adults are now smartphone owners who use their phones to look up information on a daily basis.

In response to the growing number of avenues to share information, the amount of content creators has also expanded, adding layers of complexity to the search and evaluation process. People used to be limited to reading a relatively small number of authors, scholars, journalists, and other experts, but now it is so easy and inexpensive to publish content online that the number of content creators is larger and more diverse than ever. Traditional gatekeepers to information such as editors, publishers, and producers of newspapers, magazines, books, and television are far less important than in the past. This has resulted in a virtual disappearance or devaluation of many of the processes and standards that we used to rely on to ensure information was accurate and of good quality. In many ways, individuals must now become their own gatekeepers and have to determine the quality of the information they find with little to no help, which can be much more challenging than it was when information was scarcer.[3]

---

2 Rockman, *Integrating Information Literacy into the Higher Education Curriculum: Practical Models for Transformation*, 1.

3 Urs Gasser, et al., "Youth and Digital Media: From Credibility to Information Quality," SSRN Scholarly Paper (Rochester, NY: Social Science Research Network, February 16, 2012), http://papers.ssrn.com/abstract=2005272.

INFORMED CITIZENS AND THE NETWORK SOCIETY (AND THE INFORMATION AGE)

The changes created by the rise of the Internet have resulted in what Castells calls "the network society."[4] The move from traditional mass media and old patterns and formats of communication to "a system of horizontal communication on networks organized around the Internet and wireless communication" has resulted in a "fundamental cultural transformation."[5] The Internet has become central to participation in cultural activities and civic engagement[6] and since networks are not constrained by geographic boundaries, the network society is global, so participation can potentially be more inclusive. However, it is not all inclusive as some people and places are included while others are left out, creating a new geography of social, economic, and technological inequality. Savvy information and technology use is quickly becoming a prerequisite to success in contemporary society and those who fail to learn the necessary skills are at risk of being left behind both economically and socially.

The skills and resources people need to discover truth amid the chaotic and saturated information landscape have grown in number and complexity. To be fully informed citizens, individuals must have a strong understanding of how information is created, organized, distributed, and accessed. As Boyer argues,

> ...information is...our most precious resource. In such a world, education should empower everyone, not the few. But for information to become knowledge, and ultimately, one hopes, wisdom, it must be organized. And, in this new climate, the public interest challenge, beyond access and equity is, I believe, sorting and selection. The challenge of educators is to help students make sense of a world described by some as 'information overload.'[7]

---

4   Manuel Castells, *The Rise of the Network Society, Information Age* (Malden, MA: Blackwell Publishers, 2010), 1.

5   Ibid.

6   Gasser, et al., "Youth and Digital Media."

7   Boyer, *Scholarship Reconsidered: Priorities of the Professoriate*, 140.

Educators must develop new understandings of learning and thinking so they can help students navigate the network society and respond to the rapid changes that have proven to be one of its defining characteristics. As educators and policymakers have searched for ways to help people develop the skills and knowledge necessary for success in this new environment, many librarians, teachers, and scholars have argued that teaching information literacy from kindergarten through graduate school is at least part of the answer. As Kellner and Share explain, "in our global information society, it is insufficient to teach students to read and write only with letters and numbers...[because] the majority of information people receive comes from highly constructed visual images, complex sound arrangements, and multiple media formats."[8] What it means to be a literate person has changed in the last two decades and information literacy has become a new basic literacy. In turn, "information literacy has become a central concept for academic libraries in the information age as librarians have begun to see their work as less about managing physical collections and more about helping students and faculty navigate the complex, emergent information environment."[9]

Along with librarians, leading education scholars of the twentieth and twenty-first centuries, such as Castells, Freire, Giroux, and Boyer have written on the importance of adapting education in response to the changing information landscape.[10] These scholars and others provide support for the argument that information literacy is *the* campus wide issue of this century.[11] As Bundy argued, information literacy "is a prerequisite for participative citizenship, social inclusion, the creation of new knowledge, personal empowerment, and learning for life."[12] The United Nations Educational, Scientific and Cultural

---

8   Kellner and Share, "Toward Critical Media Literacy: Core Concepts, Debates, Organizations, and Policy," 3.

9   James Elmborg, "Literacies Large and Small: The Case of Information Literacy," *International Journal of Learning* 11 (2004): 5, http://ir.uiowa.edu/slis_pubs/1/.

10 Castells, *Critical Education in the New Information Age*; Freire, *The Politics of Education: Culture, Power, and Liberation*; Giroux, "Critical Theory and Educational Practice"; Boyer, *Scholarship Reconsidered: Priorities of the Professoriate*.

11 Rockman, *Integrating Information Literacy into the Higher Education Curriculum: Practical Models for Transformation*.

12 Bundy, Australian and New Zealand Information Literacy Framework, 8.

Organization (UNESCO) and International Federation of Library Associations and Institutions (IFLA) have taken a similarly strong stance on the importance of information literacy by writing in the "Alexandria Proclamation" that:

> Information Literacy lies at the core of lifelong learning. It empowers people in all walks of life to seek, evaluate, use and create information effectively to achieve their personal, social, occupational and educational goals. It is a basic human right in a digital world and promotes social inclusion of all nations. Lifelong learning enables individuals, communities and nations to attain their goals and to take advantage of emerging opportunities in the evolving global environment for shared benefit. It assists them and their institutions to meet technological, economic and social challenges, to redress disadvantage and to advance the well-being of all.[13]

Even President Obama has weighed in, declaring October of 2009 National Information Literacy Awareness Month. He asserted that the month "highlights the need for all Americans to be adept in the skills necessary to effectively navigate the Information Age. Though we may know how to find the information we need, we must also know how to evaluate it." And further that "an informed and educated citizenry is essential to the functioning of our modern democratic society, and I encourage educational and community institutions across the country to help Americans find and evaluate the information they seek, in all its forms."[14]

Unfortunately, the big ideas that are presented as arguments for information literacy have not come to be reflected in the reality of how information literacy is actually taught and included in school and organizational goals. Most intentional information literacy instruction is taught by school and academic librarians in a hit or miss

---

13   United Nations Educational, Scientific and Cultural Organization and International Federation of Library Associations and Institutions, "Beacons of the Information Society: The Alexandria Proclamation on Information Literacy and Lifelong Learning," para. 2-3.

14   https://www.whitehouse.gov/the-press-office/presidential-proclamation-national-information-literacy-awareness-month

fashion.[15] Librarians teach whomever they can whenever they can, but are at the mercy of teachers, faculty, and administrators who often treat information literacy as something that will just magically come to students as they complete their coursework. This has led to a lot of information literacy instruction being mostly skills-focused, without including much of the higher-level thinking and critical reflection that true information literacy requires.[16]

Problematizing Information Literacy in Higher Education

Gathering and analyzing information has largely become the center of gravity in higher education. In the recent past, the material students were expected to learn was presented to them in easy-to-use prepackaged formats, such as textbooks or photocopied course packs. It is becoming less and less likely that professors will simply supply a textbook and expect their students to develop knowledge through the use of that one source. They expect them to find and use a variety of sources, making it necessary for students to develop a whole new skillset that previous generations of college students did not have to have.[17] Today's students are often expected to find their own information, supplement the information provided by professors with their own findings, and access materials from a variety of providers.

Unfortunately, numerous studies[18] have shown that most students do not enter college with these skills or learn them in their coursework. Librarians and other educators have been largely unsuccessful with teaching information literacy because of how they teach it, due to a lack of teaching skill and training, poorly devised

---

15   Nardine and Meier, "Assessing the One-Shot Instruction Session"; Wilkinson and Cairns, "Life beyond the One-Shot: Librarians Teaching a for-Credit Course."

16   Swanson, "A Radical Step: Implementing a Critical Information Literacy Model."

17   Hounsell, "Contrasting Conceptions of Essay-Writing."

18   Hart, "Rising to the Challenge: Are High School Graduates Prepared for College and Work? A Study of Recent High School Graduates, College Instructors, and Employers"; Head and Eisenberg, "How College Students Use the Web to Conduct Everyday Life Research"; Katz, "Testing Information Literacy in Digital Environments: ETS's iSkills Assessment"; Kolowich, "What Students Don't Know"; Latham and Gross, "Broken Links: Undergraduates Look Back on Their Experiences with Information Literacy in K-12 Education."

curriculum, inability to embed information literacy in the overall curriculum, and limitations of common instructional models.[19] Further, as information literacy is currently conceptualized and taught, the focus is on mechanistic, surface skills that do not provide students with a deep enough understanding of how information is produced, disseminated, and consumed. The power structures that are embedded within the entire information lifecycle are typically left out of the average information literacy instruction program, leaving students with an anemic view of how the information world really works. This means that most students leave college with the ability to find basic information and do some rudimentary evaluation, but they do not usually learn to critically evaluate and reflect on the information from the perspective of the larger sociopolitical system in which it was created and distributed.[20]

In 2000, the Association of College and Research Libraries (ACRL) published foundational standards to guide information literacy efforts in the form of the widely used *Information Literacy Competency Standards for Higher Education*, but the "standards do not adequately address the fact that knowledge is socially constructed."[21] Likewise, historical models of literacy have conceptualized it as a set of competencies and defined it as simply the ability to read and write. However, "critical literacy scholars recognize literacy as a culturally-situated phenomenon, embedded within specific social, political, and economic systems, subject to (and potentially constitutive of) the power relations and ideologies that define particular moments in history."[22] The critical element is of utmost importance to information literacy because, as Brabazon argues, "the web is large, occasionally irrelevant,…outdated and increasingly corporatized."[23] Students have to learn to use both digital content and print resources appropriately.

---

19   Fister and Eland, "Curriculum Issues in Information Literacy Instruction."

20   Accardi, Drabinski, and Kumbier, *Critical Library Instruction: Theories and Methods*; Elmborg, "Critical Information Literacy: Implications for Instructional Practice"; Hart, "Rising to the Challenge: Are High School Graduates Prepared for College and Work? A Study of Recent High School Graduates, College Instructors, and Employers."

21   Keer, "Critical Pedagogy and Information Literacy in Community Colleges," 151.

22   Accardi, Drabinski, and Kumbier, *Critical Library Instruction: Theories and Methods*, ix.

23   Brabazon, *The University of Google: Education in the (post) Information Age*, 155.

They must be taught to evaluate for credibility and quality and to ask questions of and critically reflect on the books, articles, and websites that they read.

To deal with the issues of overly simplified, mechanistic information literacy skills teaching within the context of a confusing and largely corporatized information rich world, a growing number of librarians and information literacy scholars have begun to study and teach a relatively new subset of information literacy called *critical information literacy*, which looks at the cultural, social, and economic structures that underlie all of information production and dissemination. Critical information literacy scholars and practitioners urge students to approach all information, regardless of the type or source, with a critical eye and to be reflective of their role as information consumers and producers. Many also argue that students need to go beyond critical reflection and actively disrupt dominant modes of information production in order to challenge oppressive power structures.

In addition to requiring more from students, critical information literacy also requires more from those teaching it. While "traditional information literacy as a pedagogy is objectified and externalized, its core values ('information,' 'facts,' 'knowledge') reified into book collections and databases, and its methodology instrumental,"[24] critical information literacy is grounded in praxis, which in the simplest terms is "practice informed by theory."[25] One of the first authors to advocate for critical information literacy, Cushla Kapitzke, urged librarians to embrace transformative information literacy practices, "adopt[ing] a critical perspective not only to information resources but also to [their] own practice and methodology and broaden analysis to socio-political ideologies embedded within economies of ideas and information."[26]

---

24   Kaptizke as cited in J.S. Riddle, "Information and Service Learning," in *Critical Library Instruction: Theories and Methods*, ed. Maria T. Accardi, Emily Drabinski, and Alana Kumbier (Duluth, MN: Library Juice Press, 2010), 136.

25   Hoffman, J. "Praxis." *Marxism and the Theory of Praxis*, 1975.

26   Kapitzke, as cited in Riddle, "Information and Service Learning," 137.

CURRENT STATE OF STUDENTS' INFORMATION LITERACY SKILLS

Research shows that a large majority of college-bound high school and college students are not information literate. In 2006, the Educational Testing Service (ETS) administered their ICT Literacy Assessment to 6300 students at 63 institutions. The ICT Literacy Assessment is a standardized test based on the *ACRL Information Literacy Competency Standards* and was developed under the guidance of college librarians, faculty, and administrators. On average, students were only able to answer around 50% of the questions correctly. ETS urged educators to use caution in evaluating the preliminary results based on limitations of the sampling method used, but the results are not terribly surprising and line up with findings from other recent studies. Only 49% of students could evaluate a set of websites correctly; 44% could successfully choose an appropriate research statement for a class assignment; 35% could effectively narrow a search; and only a handful of test-takers were able to adapt material for a new audience.[27] In another study in 2008, ETS tested 3000 college students and 800 high school students. Of those, only 13% were information literate according to their scores on the ICT Literacy Assessment.[28]

Project Information Literacy (PIL) has been studying students' information skills on campuses across the country since 2005. In the spring of 2010, they surveyed 8353 students to try to find out more about how students conduct everyday life research, such as keeping current on news, how they would find information on a car they wanted to buy, or how they would conduct research for a health issue. While information literacy encompasses much more than an understanding of academic research, the overwhelming majority of information literacy research is within the context of formal learning environments. PIL's research is very important for developing a better understanding of students' research skills because they look beyond the classroom, creating a much more comprehensive picture than most studies. The PIL researchers found that 95% of students used

---

27   Katz, "Testing Information Literacy in Digital Environments: ETS's iSkills Assessment."

28   Latham and Gross, "Broken Links: Undergraduates Look Back on Their Experiences with Information Literacy in K-12 Education."

Web search engines for their everyday life research; 87% asked friends and family for this type of information; 53% turned to instructors and only 14 % asked librarians.[29] Meanwhile, the National Center for Postsecondary Improvement found that only 48% of students surveyed felt confident in their ability to find information.[30]

Studies have also shown that professors do not believe that most college students are prepared to do college-level research. Achieve conducted a national survey and discovered that 59% of college instructors felt that their students were poorly prepared to do research. Self-assessments by students on these same skills provide mixed results. In the Achieve study, 40% of recent high school graduates who went on to attend college felt that they had only some gaps in their ability to do research, with 10% reporting large gaps.[31] Singh surveyed over 400 American faculty members teaching undergraduates and found that 33.8% believed their students' research skills were poor.[32]

Though finding and evaluating information underpins almost everything that students do in the current classroom, faculty and students alike do not often turn to librarians for help with these skills. Singh found that despite 55.2% of faculty reporting that they believed library instruction improved their students' research skills, only 8.6% included it in their courses.[33] Most professors expect students to either come into their classroom already possessing the skills necessary to complete research assignments or to quickly teach themselves the skills needed to accomplish these tasks. DaCosta[34] surveyed faculty in the U.S. and England to determine how important they believed information literacy skills were and to what extent they incorporated

---

29   Head and Eisenberg, "How College Students Use the Web to Conduct Everyday Life Research."

30   Rockman, *Integrating Information Literacy into the Higher Education Curriculum: Practical Models for Transformation.*

31   Hart, "Rising to the Challenge: Are High School Graduates Prepared for College and Work? A Study of Recent High School Graduates, College Instructors, and Employers."

32   Alvarez and Dimmock, "Faculty Expectations of Student Research."

33   Alvarez and Dimmock, "Faculty Expectations of Student Research."

34   DaCosta, "Is There an Information Literacy Skills Gap to Be Bridged? An Examination of Faculty Perceptions and Activities Relating to Information Literacy in the United States and England."

teaching these skills into their classes. 93% of the English and 98% of the American faculty surveyed agreed or strongly agreed that students should learn information literacy skills, but only 55% and 57% of these same professors took actions to embed learning these skills in their courses.

Studies by the California State University and the University of Rochester found that students and faculty agree that critically evaluating sources is the most difficult aspect of research for undergraduates.[35] In the PIL studies, students also said that the concept they struggle with the most is evaluating sources. They have a hard time determining which source is the "right" source and with filtering the relevant out from the irrelevant.[36] The University of Rochester study revealed that despite almost universal problems with information literacy concepts during the course of completing their research assignments, 79% did not ask a librarian for help.[37]

LIMITATIONS OF THE MAJOR INFORMATION LITERACY STANDARDS AND MODELS

In efforts to create information literate communities and societies, educators, librarians, and policymakers have created information literacy standards that provide behavioral outcomes and characteristics of information literate students to guide instruction and evaluation design. In turn, researchers and others have fleshed out the standards and developed models to define and illustrate the research and information seeking process. Models have been developed in many countries, including the United Kingdom, the United States, Canada, Scotland, Australia, and New Zealand.[38]

Most of the major information literacy instructional models in wide use today tend to focus on a set of tasks or stages and were originally developed over ten years ago. Some have been updated in the last two or three years, but most of those that originated more

---

35   Ibid.; Rockman, *Integrating Information Literacy into the Higher Education Curriculum: Practical Models for Transformation*.

36   Head and Eisenberg, "How College Students Evaluate and Use Information in the Digital Age."

37   Burns and Harper, "Asking Students about Their Research."

38   Moore, "An Analysis of Information Literacy Education Worldwide."

recently expand on older models. Whether the model is meant to be linear, cyclical, or iterative, it is thought that the student progresses through a set of steps or stages to develop competency. The models tend to focus heavily on the search process. Those that include evaluation and synthesis still do not go far enough in terms of stimulating meaningful learning. A notable exception to this is the *Framework for Information Literacy for Higher Education* published by ACRL in 2015. The *Framework* is constructed around core concepts rather than treating information literacy learning as a set of stages.[39] See Appendix A for a breakdown of the major models.

Kopp and Olson-Kopp criticized the *ACRL Information Literacy Competency Standards for Higher Education,* the most widely used IL standards in American higher education, for failing to encourage meaningful learning and critical thinking. They argued that "when learning outcomes are couched primarily in mechanistic and behavioral terms, we should not be surprised if students remain uncritical."[40] American librarians have made progress toward teaching information literacy as a rich and complex set of ideas and skills since publication of the *Framework* in early 2015, but the legacy of the *Standards* cannot be underestimated. Most of the librarians who teach information literacy in the US learned how to teach using the *Standards* as their guide and there are many librarians who do not find the *Framework* helpful or appealing and have no intention of changing their instruction in response to it.[41] Instruction librarian discussion lists have heated up with discussions of the *Framework* over the past year as librarians have debated its practicality in terms of the type of teaching and assessment they do in their institutions and the role ACRL should play in helping them activate its ideas. Chris Bombaro, Associate Director for Information Literacy and Research Services at Dickinson College wrote on the ACRLFrame listserv in late 2015:

> I've stated before on this list that we need more direction about how practically to use the Framework. The Framework

---

39   "Framework for Information Literacy for Higher Education | Association of College & Research Libraries (ACRL)."

40   Kopp and Olson-Kopp, "Depositories of Knowledge: Library Instruction and the Development of Critical Consciousness," 58.

41   Saracevic, "Information Literacy in the United States."

is quite useful as a point of discussion (and some on this list have provided great examples of that), but less so in developing goals, outcomes and assessments. This is not an issue of merely being uncomfortable with dynamic and non-linear forms of assessment. Not all academic librarians are faculty and thus do not have direct access to committees in which something like the Framework can be analyzed and adapted for the local environment. Not all have the luxury of academic leave that affords the time to sort through the issues raised by Threshold Concepts at the level of attention they demand. Therefore, it is the responsibility of ACRL to give us the guidance we're asking for.

I too have been to conferences and workshops, and participated in classes that were supposed to help us engage with the Framework. Unfortunately, none of the work that resulted from my participation in any of those experiences (or the work of others when I was able to see it) differed significantly in any way from similar exercises when the Standards were the guiding principle. In fact, what I've observed is that individuals are basically re-writing the Standards as goals or outcomes, using a Threshold Concept as a theme.

The ACRL must explain how the Framework can be more effective than the Standards. What, in practical terms, does the Framework offer me—a teacher in the classroom—that will transform my teaching in ways that the Standards did not? How can I use this to demonstrate my own effectiveness in ways that do not simply look like a re-write of the Standards? Who can show me a concrete example of how a set of goals or outcomes or an assessment plan developed using the Framework differs *fundamentally* from what the same document might have looked like when the guiding ideology was the Standards?

I know that I am not the only one with these questions. The directive that I should take the initiative to adapt the Framework to my local institution or consortium is not only frustrating, but it also places a burden of interpreting and implementing conceptual theories on academic librarians who for any number of reasons cannot meet the challenge.

Chris Bombaro
Dickinson College

At the time of this writing, the Framework–Standards debate continues in the American academic library community. Countries outside of the US have developed their own standards and models specific to their citizens, but they have not strayed far from those outlined by ACRL. For example, the Society of College, National and University Libraries (SCONUL) in Great Britain developed a model of "seven pillars" of information literacy, which outline the skills and abilities an information literate individual should possess. Unfortunately, the seven pillars "do not extend beyond the skills-based [ACRL] model of information literacy development and do not suggest a relationship between information and the values of either the information provider or the information literate person."[42]

One result of relying on standards-based models in education is that it can limit teachers' pedagogical growth. While there has "been substantial international debate and research on information literacy and there have been repeated efforts to draw up skill lists, standards, and models,"[43] the same efforts have not been put into curriculum design for information literacy or efforts to teach librarians—the primary teachers of information literacy—how to teach. Harris contended that "in some ways, the standards have taken the place of pedagogy in library instruction, resulting in a profession-wide dependence on lists of educational outcomes to define both the theory and practice of information literacy instruction."[44]

A further challenge to information literacy is that librarians alone cannot harness and deal with the huge challenges students will face in the current information landscape; this is a problem that confronts all of education. A longstanding critique of the *Standards* is that they remove information literacy from context, leading to mechanized and skills-based teaching, while also stripping information of its deeper meaning, power, and value.

---

42 Harris, "Encountering Values: The Place of Critical Consciousness in the Competency Standards," 284.

43 Johnston and Webber, "Information Literacy in Higher Education," 340.

44 B. Harris, "Encountering Values: The Place of Critical Consciousness in the Competency Standards," in *Critical Library Instruction: Theories and Methods*, ed. Maria T. Accardi, Emily Drabinski, and Alana Kumbier (Duluth, MN: Library Juice Press, 2010), 279.

One solution that has gained popularity in recent years is the idea of embedding information literacy in and across the curriculum. Although this is hardly a new concept—interestingly, the first major library instruction study published in 1966 reached this same conclusion[45]—it is gaining more support.

Some librarians have argued vehemently that information literacy instruction should be provided by librarians because they are the information experts. However, train-the-trainer models and collaborations between librarians and faculty have been shown to be more successful because librarians do not have enough direct access to students to be able to fully teach and reinforce the complexities of information literacy. Additionally, considering that the Internet and its various applications have become the "communication fabric of our lives,"[46] it is ridiculous to think teaching students to understand and use it well should be limited to only one discipline, especially a discipline with such limited reach in terms of instructional opportunities.

INTRODUCING CRITICAL INFORMATION LITERACY

While librarians have done a good job of making the case for the importance of information literacy in higher education, they have over-simplified the concepts and relied on static sets of standards and outcomes to drive their pedagogy. Meanwhile, students in study after study demonstrate that they are not information literate. Librarians have tried to combat this when and where they can, but their methods have fallen short due to lack of time with students, poor teaching skills, and a limited understanding of pedagogy. A growing number of librarians have turned to experiential education, critical pedagogy, and transformative learning theories looking for answers to help them address the complex problems posed by the continuously changing information landscape. These librarians see in information literacy the opportunity to help students transform themselves and their worlds by seeking "to develop teaching practices that [will] empower

---

45   Patricia B. Knapp and Wayne State University, *The Monteith College Library Experiment* (New York, NY: Scarecrow Press, 1966).

46   Castells, *The Rise of the Network Society*, 8.

self-directed learners who actively and critically examine information systems and accepted codes of legitimacy."[47]

John Raulston Saul asserted that a critical approach to information is more important than ever because the ruling elites have, rely on, and must control more knowledge than ever before. But while the knowledge they control is part of their power or strength, it also makes them more vulnerable. "The possession, use, and control of knowledge have become their central theme—the theme song of their expertise" but he contends that it is not their *use* of knowledge that gives them the most power. Their power comes from how effectively they control that knowledge.[48]

Critical information literacy scholars ask what role libraries do and should play in disrupting existing power structures. Elmborg has asked if "the library [is] a passive information bank where students and faculty make knowledge deposits and withdrawals, or is it a place where students engage existing knowledge and shape it to their own current and future uses?"[49] This book attempts to answer this question by exploring the state of critical information literacy in higher education as it is enacted and understood by academic librarians.

In the following chapters, I will discuss how critical information literacy fits within the context of critical education theories; describe the teaching techniques of librarians who teach critical information literacy; provide some ideas on content that works well in critical information literacy sessions; and discuss how librarians have worked to embed critical information literacy in their organization's curriculum, what methods of developing and implementing programs librarians have found successful, and what barriers—including those stemming from the librarianship profession—tend to get in the way

---

47   C. Sinkinson and M. C. Lingold, "Re-Visioning the Library Seminar through a Lens of Critical Pedagogy," in *Critical Library Instruction: Theories and Methods*, ed. Maria T. Accardi, Emily Drabinski, and Alana Kumbier (Duluth, MN: Library Juice Press, 2010), 81.

48   Edward A. Comor, *Media, Structures, and Power: The Robert E. Babe Collection* (University of Toronto Press, 2011), 220.

49   As cited in B.M. Kopp and K. Olson-Kopp, "Depositories of Knowledge: Library Instruction and the Development of Critical Consciousness," in *Critical Library Instruction: Theories and Methods*, ed. Maria T. Accardi, Emily Drabinski, and Alana Kumbier (Duluth, MN: Library Juice Press, 2010), 55.

of advancing critical information literacy efforts in higher education. My hope is that this book will give librarians and others who are interested in teaching critical information literacy the inspiration, foundational knowledge, and tools they need to get started with their own critical information literacy practice.

Works Cited

Accardi, Maria T., Emily Drabinski, and Alana Kumbier, eds. *Critical Library Instruction: Theories and Methods.* Duluth, MN: Library Juice Press, 2010.

Alvarez, B., and N. Dimmock. "Faculty Expectations of Student Research." In *Studying Students: The Undergraduate Research Project at the University of Rochester,* edited by Nancy Fried Foster and Susan Gibbons, 1-6. Chicago: Association of College and Research Libraries, 2007.

Boyer, Ernest L. *Scholarship Reconsidered: Priorities of the Professoriate.* A Special Report. Princeton, NJ: Carnegie Foundation for the Advancement of Teaching, 1997.

Brabazon, Tara. *The University of Google: Education in the (Post) Information Age.* Burlington, VT: Ashgate, 2007.

Bundy, A., ed. *Australian and New Zealand Information Literacy Framework.* 2nd ed. Adelaide, Australia: Australian and New Zealand Institute for Information Literacy, 2004. http://www. literacyhub.org/documents/InfoLiteracyFramework.pdf.

Burns, V., and K. Harper. "Asking Students about Their Research." In *Studying Students: The Undergraduate Research Project at the University of Rochester,* edited by Nancy Fried Foster and Susan Gibbons, 7-15. Chicago: Association of College and Research Libraries, 2007.

Castells, Manuel. *Critical Education in the New Information Age.* Critical Perspectives Series. Lanham, MD: Rowman & Littlefield, 1999.

———. *The Rise of the Network Society.* Information Age. Malden, MA: Blackwell Publishers, 2010.

DaCosta, Jacqui Weetman. "Is There an Information Literacy Skills Gap to Be Bridged? An Examination of Faculty Perceptions and Activities Relating to Information Literacy in the United

States and England." *College & Research Libraries* 71, no. 3 (2010): 203-22. http://crl.acrl.org/.

Dewey, John. *Democracy and Education: An Introduction to the Philosophy of Education.* New York: Macmillan, 1916.

Elmborg, James. "Critical Information Literacy: Implications for Instructional Practice." *Journal of Academic Librarianship* 32, no. 2 (2006): 192–99. http://www.journals.elsevier.com/the-journal-of-academic-librarianship/.

Fister, B., and T. Eland. "Curriculum Issues in Information Literacy Instruction." In *Information Literacy Instruction Handbook.* Chicago: Association of College and Research Libraries, 2008.

"Framework for Information Literacy for Higher Education | Association of College & Research Libraries (ACRL)." Accessed November 13, 2015. http://www.ala.org/acrl/ standards/ilframework.

Freire, Paulo. *The Politics of Education: Culture, Power, and Liberation.* Hadley, MA: Bergin & Garvey, 1985.

Gasser, Urs, Sandra Cortesi, Momin Malik, and Ashley Lee. "Youth and Digital Media: From Credibility to Information Quality." SSRN Scholarly Paper. Rochester, NY: Social Science Research Network, February 16, 2012. http://papers.ssrn.com/ abstract=2005272.

Giroux, H. A. "Critical Theory and Educational Practice." In *The Critical Pedagogy Reader*, edited by Antonia Darder, Marta Baltodano, and Rodolfo D. Torres, 27-56. New York: Routledge Falmer, 2003.

Harris, B. "Encountering Values: The Place of Critical Consciousness in the Competency Standards." In *Critical Library Instruction: Theories and Methods*, edited by Maria T. Accardi, Emily Drabinski, and Alana Kumbier. Duluth, MN: Library Juice Press, 2010.

Hart, P. D. "Rising to the Challenge: Are High School Graduates Prepared for College and Work? A Study of Recent High

School Graduates, College Instructors, and Employers," 2005. http://www.achieve.org/files/pollreport_0.pdf.

Head, A. J., and M. B. Eisenberg. "How College Students Use the Web to Conduct Everyday Life Research." *First Monday* 16, no. 4 (2011). http://journals.uic.edu/ojs/index.php/fm/index.

Head, Alison J., and Michael B. Eisenberg. "How College Students Evaluate and Use Information in the Digital Age." Seattle, WA: The Information School, 2010. http://projectinfolit. org/pdfs/PIL_Fall2010_Survey_FullReport1. Pdf

Hoffman, J. *Marxism and the Theory of Praxis*, 1975.

Hounsell, Dai. "Contrasting Conceptions of Essay-Writing." In *The Experience of Learning: Implications for Teaching and Studying in Higher Education*, edited by F. Marton, Dai Hounsell, and N. Entwhistle, 3rd ed., 106–25. Edinburgh: University of Edinburgh, Centre for Teaching, Learning and Assessment, 2005. http://www.etl.tla.ed.ac.uk/docs/ExperienceofLearning/EoL7.pdf.

Johnston, Bill, and Sheila Webber. "Information Literacy in Higher Education: A Review and Case Study." *Studies in Higher Education* 28, no. 3 (2003): 335–52. doi:10.1080/03075070309295.

Katz, I. R. "Testing Information Literacy in Digital Environments: ETS's iSkills Assessment." *Information Technology and Libraries* 26, no. 3 (2007). doi:10.6017/ital.v26i3.3271.

Keer, G. "Critical Pedagogy and Information Literacy in Community Colleges." In *Critical Library Instruction: Theories and Methods*, edited by Maria T. Accardi, Emily Drabinski, and Alana Kumbier, 149–60. Duluth, MN: Library Juice Press, 2010.

Kellner, Douglas, and Jeff Share. "Toward Critical Media Literacy: Core Concepts, Debates, Organizations, and Policy." *Discourse: Studies in the Cultural Politics of Education* 26, no. 3 (2005): 369–86. doi:10.1080/01596300500200169.

Kolowich, S. "What Students Don't Know." *Inside Higher Ed*, August 22, 2011. http://www.insidehighered.com.

Kopp, B.M., and K. Olson-Kopp. "Depositories of Knowledge: Library Instruction and the Development of Critical Consciousness." In *Critical Library Instruction: Theories and Methods*, edited by Maria T. Accardi, Emily Drabinski, and Alana Kumbier, 55-68. Duluth, MN: Library Juice Press, 2010.

Latham, Don, and Melissa Gross. "Broken Links: Undergraduates Look Back on Their Experiences with Information Literacy in K-12 Education." *School Library Media Research* 11 (2008). http://www.ala.org/aasl/slr.

Moore, Penny. "An Analysis of Information Literacy Education Worldwide." *School Libraries Worldwide* 11, no. 2 (2005). http://www.iasl-online.org/pubs/slw/.

Nardine, Jennifer, and Carolyn Meier. "Assessing the One-Shot Instruction Session: Leveraging Technology for Optimum Results." *Virginia Libraries* 56, no. 3 (September 7, 2010): 25-28. http://scholar.lib.vt.edu/ejournals/VALib/.

Riddle, J.S. "Information and Service Learning." In *Critical Library Instruction: Theories and Methods*, edited by Maria T. Accardi, Emily Drabinski, and Alana Kumbier, 133-48. Duluth, MN: Library Juice Press, 2010.

Rockman, Ilene F. *Integrating Information Literacy into the Higher Education Curriculum: Practical Models for Transformation*. Jossey-Bass Higher and Adult Education Series. San Francisco, CA: Jossey-Bass, 2004.

Saracevic, Tefko. "Information Literacy in the United States: Contemporary Transformations and Controversies." In *Information Literacy. Lifelong Learning and Digital Citizenship in the 21st Century*, 19-30. Springer, 2014. http://link.springer.com/chapter/10.1007/978-3-319-14136-7_3.

Swanson, Troy A. "A Radical Step: Implementing a Critical Information Literacy Model." *portal: Libraries and the Academy* 4, no. 2 (2004): 259-73. http://muse.jhu.edu/journals/portal_libraries_and_the_academy.

United Nations Educational, Scientific and Cultural Organization, and International Federation of Library Associations and Institutions. "Beacons of the Information Society: The Alexandria Proclamation on Information Literacy and Lifelong Learning," 2005. http://archive.ifla.org/III/wsis/BeaconInfSoc.html.

Wilkinson, Lane, and Virginia Cairns. "Life beyond the One-Shot: Librarians Teaching a for-Credit Course." *Tennessee Libraries* 60, no. 3 (2010). http://www.tnla.org/displaycommon.cfm?an=1&subarticlenbr=17.

CHAPTER 2

THE THEORETICAL FOUNDATIONS OF CRITICAL INFORMATION LITERACY

As a burgeoning field, the research and writing on critical information literacy has quickly grown in the last five years with the publication of research articles, theoretical treatments, and ideas for practical applications. But this shift was slow to come. When I started studying critical information literacy in 2009, there was only a very small body of work to draw from. James Elmborg, one of the first, and the most cited author in the area of critical information literacy, argued that the library literature "has been slow to embrace critical approaches to literacy or to integrate critical perspectives into research or practice."[1] Elmborg,[2] Leckie,[3] Eisenhower and Smith,[4] and others have argued that librarians have fallen behind other educators in both theoretical and practical terms, largely because of the historical positioning of librarianship as a neutral and technocratic profession. Due to this

---

1 James Elmborg, "Critical Information Literacy: Implications for Instructional Practice," *Journal of Academic Librarianship* 32, no. 2 (2006): 193, http://www.journals.elsevier.com/the-journal-of-academic-librarianship/.

2 James Elmborg, "Literacies Large and Small: The Case of Information Literacy," *International Journal of Learning* 11 (2004): 1235, http://ir.uiowa.edu/slis_pubs/1/.

3 Gloria J. Leckie, *Information Technology in Librarianship: New Critical Approaches* (ABC-CLIO, 2009).

4 Cathy Eisenhower and Dolsy Smith, "Discipline and Indulgence," in *Writing against the Curriculum: Anti-Disciplinarity in the Writing and Cultural Studies Classroom*, ed. Randi Gray Kristensen and Ryan M Claycomb (Lanham, MD: Lexington, 2010).

slow embrace in the library and information science literature, it is necessary to consider the body of educational theory that critical information literacy draws from in order to fully understand it.

In this chapter, I will briefly describe the major concepts that feed into the definition of critical information literacy, followed by an overview of experiential education and describe the work of two educators, Freire and Mezirow and their respective theories: critical pedagogy and transformative learning. Next I will discuss deep and meaningful learning as essential to any transformative learning process and contrast this with the surface learning approaches that are typical in information literacy instruction.

Information Literacy

It is generally agreed upon in the literature that the term 'information literacy' was first coined by Paul Zurkowski in 1974 in a paper for the US National Commission on Libraries and Information Science. Zurkowski's initial conception of information literacy was significantly different from its current iteration. His focus was on the private sector and the changing work environments in the United States.[5] In the years since Zurkowski presented the basic idea of information literacy, several major national and international organizations have developed definitions to guide their work and that of their members. All of these definitions include descriptions of some of the major skills that could be used to identify an information literate person, including being able to find, use, and evaluate information. Beyond these basics, the definitions tend to vary in how encompassing they consider information literacy to be, including differences in what is designated "information."

According to the American Library Association (ALA), "information literate people are those who have learned how to learn. They know how to learn because they know how knowledge is organized, how to find information, and how to use information in such a way that others can learn from them.(...) [T]hey can always

---

5   Patricia Davitt Maughan, "Assessing Information Literacy among Undergraduates: A Discussion of the Literature and the University of California-Berkeley Assessment Experience," *College & Research Libraries* 62, no. 1 (January 1, 2001): 71-85, http://crl. acrl.org/content/62/1/71.

find the information needed for any task or decision at hand."[6] The Society of College, National and University Libraries (SCONUL) define information literacy as "an umbrella term which encompasses concepts such as digital, visual, and media literacies, academic literacy, information handling, information skills, data curation, and data management."[7] UNESCO defined it more "broadly…as the ability to access and use a variety of information sources to solve an information need. Yet, it can also be defined as the development of a complex set of critical skills that allow people to express, explore, question, communicate and understand the flow of ideas among individuals and groups in quickly changing technological environments."[8]

Beyond the major definitions that have gained approval from national and international organizations, many individual scholars have also developed useful definitions of information literacy. Babu argued that it is a "natural extension of the concept of literacy" in our information society and is "pivotal to the pursuit of lifelong learning."[9] This clearly articulates that information literacy has become a new basic and essential literacy in the twenty-first century. The most well-rounded and complete definition I have identified in the literature and the one that will guide this work comes from Bundy:

> Information literacy is an intellectual framework for recognizing the need for, understanding, finding, evaluating, and using information. These are activities which may be supported in part by fluency with information technology, in part by sound investigative methods, but most importantly through critical discernment and reasoning. Information literacy initiates, sustains, and extends lifelong

---

6   American Library Association, "Presidential Committee on Information Literacy: Final Report," 1989, para. 3, http://www.ala.org/acrl/publications/whitepapers/presidential.

7   SCONUL Working Group on Information Literacy, "The SCONUL Seven Pillars of Information Literacy: Core Model for Higher Education," 2011, 3.

8   United Nations Educational, Scientific and Cultural Organization, "Information Literacy," 2009, 150, http://portal.unesco.org/ci/en/ev.php-URL_ID=27055&URL_DO=DO_TOPIC&URL_SECTION=201.html.

9   B. R. Babu, "Information Literacy Competency Standards and Performance Indicators: An Overview," *DESIDOC Journal of Library & Information Technology* 28, no. 2 (2008): 56, http://publications.drdo.gov.in/ojs/index.php/djlit/index.

learning through abilities that may use technologies but are ultimately independent of them.[10]

WHAT INFORMATION LITERACY IS NOT

Information literacy is often confused with computer literacy and information retrieval. These two skill sets, while they can inform information literacy, are very different. Computer literacy and information retrieval are focused on the technical aspects of using technology and finding information while information literacy is focused on the content found with the technology and information retrieval systems. Information and library literacy are also often confused with one another or used interchangeably. Library literacy and information retrieval are much narrower in scope than information literacy.

Shapiro and Hughes "recognize and point out the differences between information literacy and computer use, noting 'information and computer literacy, in the conventional sense are functionally valuable technical skills. But information literacy should in fact be conceived more broadly as a new liberal art that extends from knowing how to use computers and access information to critical reflection on the nature of information itself, its technical infrastructure, and its social, cultural, and even philosophical context and impact – as essential to the mental framework of the educated information-age citizen as the trivium of basic liberal arts (grammar, logic, and rhetoric) was to the educated person in medieval society.'"[11]

Information Retrieval (IR) skills are also often confused with information literacy skills. Computer-based IR has been a field since the 1940s; it is much more technical and focused on a limited set of skills, mostly involving search. While search and retrieval have been a focus of research and development for several decades, it is only in the recent past that search has become a well-known and

---

10   A. Bundy, ed., *Australian and New Zealand Information Literacy Framework*, 2nd ed. (Adelaide, Australia: Australian and New Zealand Institute for Information Literacy, 2004), 4, http://www.literacyhub.org/documents/InfoLiteracyFramework.pdf.

11   As cited in Ilene F. Rockman, *Integrating Information Literacy into the Higher Education Curriculum: Practical Models for Transformation*, Jossey-Bass Higher and Adult Education Series (San Francisco, CA: Jossey-Bass, 2004), 7.

oft discussed topic of the global brain. Nonetheless, what is now commonly termed search (i.e. "Google has a monopoly on the development of search" or "students must learn how search works to be successful in today's world.") is interchangeable with IR. These skills run the gamut from low-technical to highly technical, with information seeking on one end of the continuum and compression and algorithms on the other.

Information literacy has a much wider scope than library literacy. Information exists in a variety of formats all around us. It cannot all be found in the library and the majority of students do not use the library to find the information they need for their coursework. Therefore, focusing only on library literacy rather than sharing our knowledge of the much larger information world does students a disservice and does not adequately prepare them for success. Li and Lester argued that "we need to teach students adaptable, transferrable skills for accessing, utilizing, and synthesizing multi-format and multimedia information across heterogeneous applications, databases, and systems."[12]

INFORMATION

Scholars[13] have challenged the definitions of information literacy written by ALA and ACRL because they did not define "information" prior to defining "information literacy." They argued that it is impossible to determine what makes someone literate in something without first defining what that something is. At its most basic, "information means interpreted data, news or facts."[14] More expansively, "information can be anything around us, such as breaking news, codes, events, images, names, numbers, pictures, signals, signs, tables, texts, and so on."[15] Elmborg agreed

---

12   LiLi Li and Lori Lester, "Rethinking Information Literacy Instructions in the Digital Age," *International Journal of Learning* 16, no. 11 (2009): 572, http://ijl.cgpublisher.com/product/pub.30/prod.1994.

13   Li and Lester, "Rethinking Information Literacy Instructions in the Digital Age"; Elmborg, "Literacies Large and Small."

14   Bundy, *Australian and New Zealand Information Literacy Framework*, 9.

15   Li and Lester, "Rethinking Information Literacy Instructions in the Digital Age," 571.

that information should be defined prior to defining information literacy and provides his own definition, which focuses on the social nature of information. He argued it is "the product of socially negotiated epistemological processes and the raw material for the further making of new knowledge."[16] For the purposes of this book, information encompasses all of the above. It includes data, texts, images, news, facts, and so forth and it is socially constructed.

LITERACY

If it is important to define "information" before trying to develop an understanding of information literacy, it makes sense to define "literacy" as well. "Literacy is conventionally the ability to read, but increasingly has become associated with the ability to understand or to interpret specific phenomena."[17] Therefore, in the broadest sense, literacy is being "knowledgeable or educated in a particular field or fields."[18] However, scholars have written on and debated the meaning of literacy and how it relates to education and knowledge so extensively that this broad definition overly simplifies the concept as it is used in the academic literature. To try to reconcile the many definitions of literacy used across disciplines, UNESCO highlighted "four discrete understandings of literacy: literacy as an autonomous set of skills; literacy as applied, practiced and situated; literacy as a learning process; and literacy as text."[19]

While the common usage of the term literacy primarily means the ability to read and write, it has evolved far beyond simply letters. "For a long time writing provided the only medium for preserving and transferring information beyond the face-to-face oral tradition. To know letters meant to be literate, learned. This meaning might be

---

16   Elmborg, "Critical Information Literacy: Implications for Instructional Practice," 198.

17   Bundy, *Australian and New Zealand Information Literacy Framework*, 9.

18   United Nations Educational, Scientific and Cultural Organization, "Education for All: Literacy for Life" (Paris, France: United Nations Educational, Scientific and Cultural Organization, 2005), 148, http://www.ungei.org/resources/index_581.html.

19   Ibid.

described as a level one meaning of literacy,"[20] but a more accurate definition of literacy should include more than just written text. It is the "ability to read, interpret, and produce 'texts' appropriate and valued within a given community." In this sense, "texts" means "anything that can be read and interpreted."[21]

Further, the idea of literacy as being dichotomous in nature has also evolved. Most literacy experts no longer conceive of an individual as either "literate" or "illiterate," but rather see literacy as a continuum.[22] Some of the above definitions of information and literacy touch on the cultural and social aspects of the concepts, but they do not delve deeply enough into the criticality that critical theorists think should be included in conversations about information and literacy.

CRITICAL LITERACY

The prime function of education is to create knowledge and truth[23] and learning to read texts, images, media, and other documents is fundamentally about learning to understand the meaning of such things in order to develop knowledge and find truth. Foucault and Gordon argued that "the exercise of power perpetually creates knowledge and conversely knowledge constantly induces effects of power."[24] Critical literacy instruction encourages students to analyze the power structures underlying the texts under study in an equitable and empowering learning environment.

---

20 James W. Marcum, "Rethinking Information Literacy," *Library Quarterly* 72, no. 1 (2002): 13, http://www.press.uchicago.edu/ucp/journals/journal/lq.html.

21 Elmborg, "Critical Information Literacy: Implications for Instructional Practice," 195.

22 D. Bawden, "Information and Digital Literacies: A Review of Concepts," *Journal of Documentation* 57, no. 2 (2001).

23 Stephen Brookfield, *The Power of Critical Theory: Liberating Adult Learning and Teaching*, Jossey-Bass Higher and Adult Education Series (San Francisco, CA: Jossey-Bass, 2005).

24 Michel Foucault and Colin Gordon, *Power/knowledge: Selected Interviews and Other Writings, 1972-1977* (New York: Pantheon, 1980), 52.

Critical theorists argue that all of teaching embraces and reinforces a specific perspective or belief system[25] because both students and teacher are a part of their social and cultural system and what transpires between them takes place within that context. To argue that teaching can be neutral is false and misleading. That which is supposedly neutral typically reinforces the status quo and supports the power structures already in place. Therefore critical literacy may be defined as "learning to read and write as part of the process of becoming conscious of one's experience as historically constructed within specific power relations."[26]

According to Shor, "critical literacy [is] for questioning power relations, discourses, and identities in a world not yet finished, just, or humane [and] challenges the status quo in an effort to discover alternative paths for self and social development."[27] Shor's definition combines the personal with the communal so that critical literacy learning is about the internal reflective process of the students' personal understandings along with the analysis of power structures in their communities and society. Therefore the critically literate student is both "reflective and reflexive: language use and education are social practices used to critically study all social practices including the social practices of language use and education."[28]

The final component of critical literacy is that it leads to social activism or change. In his seminal 1936 essay defining critical theory, Horkheimer argued that critical theory can only be judged as successful if it ends in revolutionary change. Brookfield contended that critical theory is "full of activist intent."[29] Critical

---

25   Douglas Kellner, "Toward a Critical Theory of Education," *Democracy & Nature: The International Journal of Inclusive Democracy* 9, no. 1 (March 2003), http://www.democracynature.org/.

26   Anderson and Irvine as cited in Ira Shor, "What Is Critical Literacy?," *Journal for Pedagogy, Pluralism & Practice* 4, no. 1 (1999): para. 3, http://www.lesley.edu/journal-pedagogy-pluralism-practice/.

27   Ibid., paras. 1–2.

28   Ibid., para. 24.

29   Brookfield, *The Power of Critical Theory: Liberating Adult Learning and Teaching*, 350.

literacy falls under the wider critical theory umbrella and has the same aim, as does critical information literacy.

CRITICAL INFORMATION LITERACY

The theory of critical information literacy is still being constructed and there is no fully developed and agreed upon definition. My working definition comes from layering the ideas of several information literacy scholars and librarians, using praxis as a starting point. Praxis is an essential element of the critical information literacy definition because critical theoretical tradition dictates that "theory and practice are both vital parts of a critical whole."[30] Practicing librarians and library scholars often bemoan the almost total separation of research and theory from everyday practice in libraries.[31] Library research and theoretical development is often considered the domain of graduate library schools, while librarians are so enmeshed in their day-to-day work, or practice, that they either do not have the time or do not take the time to study the theoretical underpinnings that would ideally inform their work. Praxis connects theory and practice, which is "vital to information literacy since it simultaneously strives to ground theoretical ideas into practicable activities and use experiential knowledge to rethink and re-envision theoretical concepts."[32]

So critical information literacy starts with "a library instruction praxis that promotes critical engagement with information sources, considers students collaborators in knowledge production practices (and creators in their own right), recognizes the affective dimensions

30 J. Cope, "Information Literacy and Social Power," in *Critical Library Instruction: Theories and Methods*, ed. Maria T. Accardi, Emily Drabinski, and Alana Kumbier (Duluth, MN: Library Juice Press, 2010), 15.

31 Martha Stortz, "Academicism versus Professionalism in LIS Programs," *Public Services Quarterly* 8, no. 1 (2012): 86–90, doi:10.1080/15228959.2012.650565.

32 Heidi L.M. Jacobs, "Posing the Wikipedia 'Problem': Information Literacy and the Praxis of Problem-Posing in Library Instruction," in *Critical Library Instruction: Theories and Methods*, ed. Maria T. Accardi, Emily Drabinski, and Alana Kumbier (Duluth, MN: Library Juice Press, 2010), 181.

of research, and (in some cases) has liberatory aims."[33] In addition, it must take into account the complex power relationships that undergird all of information, including its creation, presentation, storage, retrieval, and accessibility. "Most discussions of [information literacy] stress the development of applied skills that assume a rational, unconstrained, information-seeking agent operating in an environment free of social hierarchies," but "a critical [information literacy] will see information-seeking as situated within particular contexts."[34]

Critical information literacy looks beyond the strictly functional, competency-based role of information discovery and use, going deeper than the traditional conceptions of information literacy that focus almost wholly on mainstream sources and views. It "seek[s] to develop students' capacity for social questioning and act to denaturalize the social structures and world views they inhabit."[35] Further, it does not focus on "assessable objectives[, and instead urges students] to question the social, political, and economic forces involved in the creation, transmission, reception, and use of information. Ultimately, this deployment of critical pedagogy should result in information literate activity that recognizes the complicity of the individual— and the individual as a community member—in information-based power structures and struggles."[36]

THE UMBRELLA OF EXPERIENTIAL EDUCATION THEORIES AND CONCEPTS

Critical information literacy is grounded in experiential education theories and practice, which stem from the tradition of critical theory. In the broadest sense, theories that seek to emancipate individuals from any circumstances of domination or oppression are critical.

---

33 Maria T. Accardi, Emily Drabinski, and Alana Kumbier, eds., *Critical Library Instruction: Theories and Methods* (Duluth, MN: Library Juice Press, 2010), xiii.

34 Cope, "Information Literacy and Social Power," 15.

35 Ibid., 19.

36 B. Harris, "Encountering Values: The Place of Critical Consciousness in the Competency Standards," in *Critical Library Instruction: Theories and Methods*, ed. Maria T. Accardi, Emily Drabinski, and Alana Kumbier (Duluth, MN: Library Juice Press, 2010), 279.

Specific to education, this means that "critically oriented researchers attempt to understand processes in education in relation to their cultural, economic and political context."[37] Critical theory is more important than ever in education because of the changes in technology and information. Kellner argued that "emergent technologies and literacies require a careful rethinking of education in literacy in response to its new challenges that will involve an era of Deweyan experimental education, trial and error, and research and discovery."[38]

Two major theories of experiential education are critical pedagogy and transformative learning. There is some overlap between critical pedagogy and transformative learning such that some transformative approaches are considered a part of the critical pedagogical tradition and some stand alone under the experiential education umbrella (see Figure 1). Meaningful learning is an essential component to critical pedagogy and transformative learning and infuses my understanding of critical information literacy.

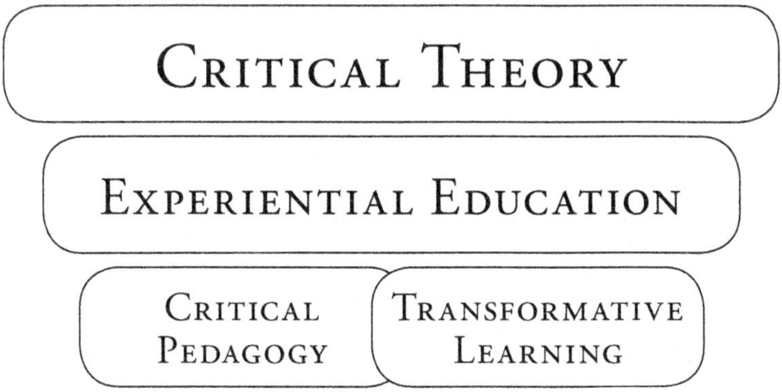

Figure 1: Educational Critical Theory Umbrella

---

37   Joseph J. Ferrare, "Can Critical Education Research Be 'Quantitative'?," in *The Routledge International Handbook of Critical Education*, ed. Michael W. Apple, Wayne Au, and Luis Armando Gandin (New York: Routledge, 2009), 465.

38   Kellner, "Toward a Critical Theory of Education," 60.

Experiential education, critical pedagogy, and transformative learning are sometimes used interchangeably and sometimes treated as complementary. Just as with critical theory, concrete definitions of any of these are hard to formulate and depend a great deal on the interpretation of the particular author or theorist writing the definition. For example, Apple, Au, and Gandin argued that critical pedagogy has become a "sliding signifier" that "seems to have been used in such broad ways that it can mean almost anything from cooperative classrooms with somewhat more political content, to a more robust definition that involves a thorough-going reconstruction of what education is for, how it should be carried out, what we should teach, and who should be empowered to engage in it."[39] Likewise, "the notion of experiential learning has been used to refer to everything from kinesthetic, directed instructional activities in the classroom to special workplace projects interspersed with 'critical dialogue' led by a facilitator to learning generated through social action movements, and even to team-building adventures in the wilderness. Definitional problems continue when one tries to disentangle the notion of experiential learning from experiences commonly associated with formal education, such as class discussions, reading and analysis, and reflection."[40] The following definitions stay as true as possible to the original ideas behind each of these concepts, while also reflecting the positive revisions that have resulted from continued study:

"*Experiential education* is a philosophy and methodology in which educators purposefully engage with learners in direct experience and focused reflection in order to increase knowledge, develop skills and clarify values."[41]

"*Critical pedagogy* is a way of thinking about, negotiating, and transforming the relationship among classroom teaching, the production of knowledge, the institutional structures of the school,

---

39   Michael W. Apple, Wayne Au, and Luís Armando Gandin, *The Routledge International Handbook of Critical Education* (Routledge, 2009), 3.

40   Tara J. Fenwick, "Expanding Conceptions of Experiential Learning: A Review of the Five Contemporary Perspectives of Cognition," *Adult Education Quarterly* 50, no. 4 (August 2000): 2, doi:10.1177/07417130022087035.

41   Association for Experiential Education, "What Is Experiential Education?," n.d., para. 3, http://www.aee.org/about/whatIsEE.

and the social and material relations of the wider community, school, and nation state."[42]

"*Transformative learning* involves a process of disorientation, critical reflection on assumptions, dialogue, and action on new meaning perspectives."[43]

EXPERIENTIAL EDUCATION

Dewey was the first major proponent of experiential learning, which he defined and explained in his classic book *Experience and Education*.[44] He argued that education should be based on learning by doing and that educators need to help students connect their past experience and knowledge to new experiences. Further, he believed students should actually do something in their environment to test out and solidify what they have learned with the new experience. All subsequent experiential learning theories and approaches have built on Dewey's work.

Since Dewey published *Experience and Education*, experiential theories and practice in education have exploded. There are so many theories and schools of thought that define themselves as falling under the experiential learning umbrella that scholars have begun to try to organize the various perspectives and approaches to make talking about and understanding this body of work manageable. Different authors have developed various categorizations for experiential learning. Fenwick divided it into four categories, including psychoanalytic, situative, critical cultural, and enactivist; Jarvinen argued for three categories, including phenomenological, critical theory, and situated and action theory; and Saddington said there were three categories, including progressive, humanist, and radical.[45] All three of these

---

42   Peter McLaren as cited in Joan Wink, *Critical Pedagogy: Notes from the Real World*, 2nd ed. (New York: Longman, 2000), 31.

43   Judith Stevens-Long, Steven A. Schapiro, and Charles McClintock, "Passionate Scholars: Transformative Learning in Doctoral Education," *Adult Education Quarterly* 62, no. 2 (May 2012): 184, doi:10.1177/0741713611402046.

44   John Dewey, *Experience and Education*, The Kappa Delta Pi Lecture Series, no. 10 (New York: Macmillan, 1938).

45   Tara J. Fenwick, "Experiential Learning: A Theoretical Critique from Five Perspectives," Information Series No. 385 (Columbus, OH: ERIC Clearinghouse on Adult, Career, and Vocational Education, 2001), http://eric.ed.gov/?id=ED454418.

schemas include a category for the type of experiential learning we are most concerned about here, which is the critical approach. The respective authors named this approach critical cultural, critical theory, and radical, which I refer to as the critical approach in this book.

Two major experiential learning theorists who have influenced the development of critical information literacy are Paulo Freire and Jack Mezirow, both of whom focused their work on adult education. Mezirow and Freire grounded their approaches in critical theory and focused on power relationships, reflection, and the emancipatory potential of education, which closely align with the goals of critical information literacy.[46]

CRITICAL PEDAGOGY

Freire is one of the best-known figures in experiential learning and is the educational theorist most embraced by critical information literacy scholars and practitioners. In his classic book *Pedagogy of the Oppressed*, he introduced critical pedagogy to educators all over the world, describing the critical pedagogical methods he used to teach Brazilian peasants to read and write. He strongly opposed teaching literacy with a mechanistic approach because he argued that it strips people of their ability to question the world around them and leads to them simply accepting dominant worldviews and assumptions. Freire called this mechanistic approach the "banking" concept of education, in which the educator deposits knowledge into the student and ideas and content are presented as static, concrete, and not open for question or interpretation. Banking education focuses on recording, memorizing, and repeating. To Freire, this type of education is meaningless and repressive.[47]

The goal of education using critical pedagogy is liberation and the process to get there is by guiding students to become critical of their thoughts, society, education, power, and so on. Freire thought the process of individuals becoming more critical of the world around

---

46 Eamon Tewell, "A Decade of Critical Information Literacy: A Review of the Literature," *Communications in Information Literacy* 9, no. 1 (2015): 24-43, http://eprints.rclis.org/28163/.

47 Paulo Freire, *Pedagogy of the Oppressed*, New rev. 20th-Anniversary ed (New York: Continuum, 1993).

them was akin to them waking up or becoming conscious. He called this process "conscientization," which he believed would lead to transformation of the individual and society. According to Freire, transformation through conscientization is what makes education meaningful.[48]

TRANSFORMATIVE LEARNING

Transformative learning focuses on the meaning structures that we have, use, and revise in the process of learning. It addresses how our experiences shift and change within the framework of our cultural assumptions and understandings, which are often called "frames of reference." Mezirow defined these as "structures of assumptions and expectations that frame an individual's tacit points of view and influence their thinking, beliefs, and actions."[49] Frames of reference serve as the container for the transformative process. The heart of transformative learning is "to raise consciousness and then to critically reflect on assumptions"[50] and to revise a frame of reference, resulting in "a more fully developed (more functional) frame of reference . . . one that is more inclusive, differentiating, permeable, critically reflective, and integrative of experience."[51]

Mezirow's work on experiential emancipatory learning also recognized change as evidence of learning. He conceived emancipatory learning as a process of critical self-awareness where the learner begins to critically evaluate and reflect on why they see a situation or an event the way they do and then critique their assumptions and values regarding their understanding of that event. He said this reflection is typically the result of a disorienting dilemma and is what provides the meaning to learning. Mezirow argued that educators

---

48   Ibid.; A. L. Wilson and L. Burket, "What Makes Learning Meaningful?" (Annual Meeting of the American Association for Adult and Continuing Education, Atlantic City, NJ, 1989), http://eric.ed.gov/?id=ED313586.

49   Edward Taylor, "Transformative Learning Theory," *New Directions in Adult and Continuing Education*, no. 119 (2008): 5, doi:10.1002/ace.

50   Elizabeth J. Tisdell, "Critical Media Literacy and Transformative Learning Drawing on Pop Culture and Entertainment Media in Teaching for Diversity in Adult Higher Education," *Journal of Transformative Education* 6, no. 1 (January 1, 2008): 51, doi:10.1177/1541344608318970.

51   Taylor, "Transformative Learning Theory," 5–6.

have a responsibility to help learners transform and emancipate their thinking, which goes far beyond simple subject matter mastery. Achieving emancipatory learning requires different teaching methods than what is required to teach students how to perform a task.[52]

Mezirow was influenced by Freire, which is clearly seen in the similarities between his perspective transformation and conscientization. Mezirow defined perspective transformation as "the process of becoming critically aware of how and why our presuppositions have come to constrain the way we perceive, understand, and feel about our world; of reformulating these assumptions to permit a more inclusive, discriminating, permeable, and integrative perspective; and of making decisions or otherwise acting upon these new understandings."[53] See Table 1 for a comparison of the main ideas of transformative learning and critical pedagogy.

	TRANSFORMATIVE LEARNING	CRITICAL PEDAGOGY
GOAL OF EDUCATION	Transformation and emancipation (individual)	Liberation (individual and society)
EVIDENCE OF LEARNING	Change in thinking based on critical evaluation and reflection on self within society (frames of reference)	Change in thinking based on critical evaluation and reflection on self and society
EVIDENCE OF CRITICAL REFLECTION	Perspective transformation	Conscientization
WHAT MAKES EDUCATION MEANINGFUL?	Reflection	Transformation
INEFFECTIVE METHODS		Mechanistic, banking

Table 1: Comparison of Transformative Learning and Critical Pedagogy

One of the main criticisms of Mezirow's conception of transformative learning is that it is too focused on the individual learner and their singular perspective. Since Mezirow first introduced his theory of transformative learning in 1978, his ideas have been expanded on

---

52   Wilson and Burket, "What Makes Learning Meaningful?"

53   Peter Jarvis, *Paradoxes of Learning: On Becoming an Individual in Society*, Jossey-Bass Higher and Adult Education Series (San Francisco, CA: Jossey-Bass, 1992), 97.

and theorists and practitioners have developed alternate perspectives of how they believe it should be conceptualized. One of these different perspectives is the "social-emancipatory" view, which is grounded in the work of Paulo Freire. While the goal of Mezirow's transformative learning approach is personal transformation, the goal of the social-emancipatory approach is social transformation. The social-emancipatory approach could also be called a critical pedagogy of transformative learning and illustrates where the overlap of critical pedagogy and transformative learning is likely to occur.[54]

The meshing of critical pedagogy and transformative learning, or the social-emancipatory approach, is a very close match for the goals of critical information literacy as they have been articulated in its short history. Kos and Spiranec argue that transformative learning should serve as the theoretical framework for critical information literacy because they both:

- acknowledge the focus on transformation (personal or social),
- aim to empower for autonomous critical thinking,
- claim they view learning as experiential and contextual,
- claim to understand meaning as negotiated and intersubjective,
- confront the possibility to be used for the purpose of dehumanization,
- have been influenced by Paulo Freire's view of education and Habermas's theory of communicative action,
- note the value and the need for critical reflection,
- and seek to define critical and reflective pedagogical practices.[55]

---

54 Taylor, "Transformative Learning Theory."

55 Denis Kos and Sonja Špiranec, "Debating Transformative Approaches to Information Literacy Education: A Critical Look at the Transformative Learning Theory," in *Information Literacy. Lifelong Learning and Digital Citizenship in the 21st Century*, ed. Serap Kurbanoğlu et al., Communications in Computer and Information Science 492 (Springer International Publishing, 2014), 427–35, http://link.springer.com/chapter/10.1007/978-3-319-14136-7_45.

Deep and Meaningful vs. Surface Learning

Transformative learning depends on pedagogy that requires the learner to delve deeply rather than focusing on teaching surface skills. Many scholars have investigated the difference between deep and surface learning, what leads to deep and meaningful learning, and why recognizing the difference is important. Experiential learning theorists in particular have spent considerable time investigating what makes learning meaningful. While "deep learning" and "meaningful learning" are not necessarily synonymous, learning does have to be meaningful to be deep. Therefore it is reasonable to look more closely at what experiential theorists have identified as the characteristics of meaningful and deep learning. These theorists argue that experience is a necessary and central component of meaningful learning and use the individual's real world experience as a starting place for learning.[56]

Jarvis and Ausubel are two experiential learning theorists who have studied the characteristics of deep and meaningful learning as opposed to surface learning. For Jarvis, "learning and action are inextricably intertwined"[57] and "learning is always an individual process: that individual change is indicative of learning, and that non-learning is reinforcement or the absence of change."[58] Jarvis's model contributes to our understanding of deep versus surface learning in particular because he argues that any experience can lead to either learning or non-learning, even experiences within an educational setting. He argued that memorization on its own leads to non-learning if the other steps in the learning process are ignored. Non-learning is the potential outcome of any experience that is deemed unimportant, not given consideration, or rejected because the learning is trivial. Jarvis contended that the evidence of learning is change and a lack of change indicates non-learning. Further, he equated meaningful learning with reflective learning.[59]

---

56   Wilson and Burket, "What Makes Learning Meaningful?"

57   Jarvis, *Paradoxes of Learning: On Becoming an Individual in Society*, 69.

58   David B. Hay, "Using Concept Maps to Measure Deep, Surface and Non-Learning Outcomes," *Studies in Higher Education* 32, no. 1 (February 2007): 41, doi:10.1080/03075070601099432.

59   Hay, "Using Concept Maps to Measure Deep, Surface and Non-Learning Outcomes"; Jarvis, *Paradoxes of Learning: On Becoming an Individual in Society*.

Like Freire and Mezirow, Jarvis situated learning within the social context of the learner and he reasoned that it is the educator's responsibility to take into account the social past that learners bring with them to the classroom. While a disjuncture between past experience and current experience are necessary for learning to occur, gaps that are too wide prevent learning. Therefore, the teacher must bridge cultural boundaries and remain mindful of gaps in experience.[60]

Ausubel viewed learning as a process of assimilating new concepts with existing concepts on a continuum from rote to meaningful. Rote learning occurs when students memorize information without trying to relate or integrate the information into their existing knowledge structures, which is similar to Jarvis's description of non-reflective learning. Meaningful learning is at the other end of the continuum and occurs when students build substantial relationships between existing knowledge structures and newly acquired information. Meaningful learning results in the assimilation of new concepts and the building of new conceptual structures.[61]

Meaningful learning approaches are typically left out of academic librarians' work on information literacy, both in theory and practice.[62] A major reason for this in practice is that most information literacy is taught in one hour or less class sessions at the discretion and mercy of teaching faculty.[63] It is very difficult to delve deeply into a complicated and multifaceted topic like information literacy in such a short period of time. Librarians have to decide what the students need to know for the research-related assignments for that specific

---

60   Wilson and Burket, "What Makes Learning Meaningful?"

61   Joseph Donald Novak, *Learning How to Learn* (New York: Cambridge University Press, 1984); E. Taricani, "Influences of Concept Mapping and Learning Styles on Learning," in *Annual Proceedings of Selected Research and Development Papers* (Annual National Convention of the Association for Educational Communications and Technology, Denver, CO, 2000).

62   B.M. Kopp and K. Olson-Kopp, "Depositories of Knowledge: Library Instruction and the Development of Critical Consciousness," in *Critical Library Instruction: Theories and Methods*, ed. Maria T. Accardi, Emily Drabinski, and Alana Kumbier (Duluth, MN: Library Juice Press, 2010), 55–68.

63   Jerilyn R. Veldof, *Creating the One-Shot Library Workshop: A Step-by-Step Guide* (Chicago: American Library Association, 2006).

class and provide information on those resources.[64] This means most library instruction sessions are not true information literacy sessions. Rather, they are resource-based and only skim the very surface of what students need to know for lifelong success.

Most librarians agree that "this approach is 'broken,'"[65] but it is often the best option available to them. Mokhtar, Majid, and Foo found in a study of 479 students that "information literacy competencies cannot be sufficiently learned and applied when the competencies are learned through one-time training, such as lecture-tutorials and, workshops, or hands-on sessions. The competencies need to be reinforced through close coaching or mediated learning so that students can identify their learning gaps, rectify them, and improve their learning under the close supervision and guidance of an expert."[66] Researchers have also investigated undergraduate students' perceptions of information using phenomenographical research methodologies to determine how students experience information and information seeking in order to design instruction more in line with students' information literacy needs. [67] Their studies revealed "that undergraduate students experience information use in a complex, multi-tiered way that needs to be addressed by higher

---

64 C. Sinkinson and M. C. Lingold, "Re-Visioning the Library Seminar through a Lens of Critical Pedagogy," in *Critical Library Instruction: Theories and Methods*, ed. Maria T. Accardi, Emily Drabinski, and Alana Kumbier (Duluth, MN: Library Juice Press, 2010), 81–88.

65 E. Peterson, "Problem-Based Learning as Teaching Strategy," in *Critical Library Instruction: Theories and Methods*, ed. Maria T. Accardi, Emily Drabinski, and Alana Kumbier (Duluth, MN: Library Juice Press, 2010), 72.

66 Intan Azura Mokhtar, Shaheen Majid, and Schubert Foo, "Information Literacy Education: Applications of Mediated Learning and Multiple Intelligences," *Library & Information Science Research* 30, no. 3 (September 2008): 99, doi:10.1016/j.lisr.2007.12.004.

67 C. Bruce, *The Seven Faces of Information Literacy* (Adelaide, Australia: Auslib Press, 1997); Clarence Maybee, "Undergraduate Perceptions of Information Use: The Basis for Creating User-Centered Student Information Literacy Instruction," *Journal of Academic Librarianship* 32, no. 1 (2006): 79-85, http://www.journals.elsevier.com/the-journal-of-academic-librarianship/; L. Limberg, "Three Conceptions of Information Seeking and Use," in *Exploring the Contexts of Information Behaviour*, ed. T. D. Wilson and D. K. Allen (London: Taylor Graham, 1999), 116-35.Australia: Auslib Press, 1997

educators when creating information literacy pedagogy,"[68] illustrating
that information literacy instruction needs to encompass more than
most of the current information literacy models suggest with their
focus on simple lists of skills.

Conclusion: Librarians and Educational Theory

Librarians do not typically learn about pedagogy or educational
theory in their coursework, yet those working in academic libraries are
increasingly required to teach students information literacy skills.[69]
Lack of training presents a serious obstacle to creating and delivering
an effective or theoretically based information literacy curriculum.
As accidental teachers, most teaching librarians are self-taught,[70]
relying on reading books, articles, and websites, and attending very
focused conference sessions rather than learning in the classroom
from experts or having the luxury of spending time fully engaged
with the theoretical understandings of teaching and learning prior to
being thrown in front of a class.

In turn, little actual research has been done on approaches
to teaching information literacy. The literature is abundant with
examples of "what worked" and how-to articles and research on
students' information literacy and library research skills. But rigorous
research connecting specific pedagogical approaches and techniques
to information literacy competencies is limited. "Existing studies on
[information literacy] have mainly focused on students' information

---

68   Maybee, "Undergraduate Perceptions of Information Use: The Basis for Creating
      User-Centered Student Information Literacy Instruction," 83.

69   Association of College and Research Libraries, "Information Literacy and
      Accreditation Agencies," 2011, http://www.ala.org/acrl/issues/infolit/standards/
      accred/accreditation; Middle States Commission on Higher Education, *Developing
      Research & Communication Skills: Guidelines for Information Literacy in the Curriculum*
      (Philadelphia, PA: Middle States Commission on Higher Education, 2003), https://
      www.msche.org/publications/Developing-Skills080111151714.pdf; Laura Saunders,
      "Regional Accreditation Organizations' Treatment of Information Literacy:
      Definitions, Collaboration, and Assessment," *Journal of Academic Librarianship* 33,
      no. 3 (2007): 317-26, http://www.journals.elsevier.com/the-journal-of-academic-
      librarianship/.

70   Scott Walter, Lori Arp, and Beth S. Woodard, "Instructional Improvement," *Reference
      & User Services Quarterly* 45, no. 3 (Spring 2006): 213-18, http://rusa.metapress.com/
      content/gl6570020747/.

skills, students' library skills, student learning outcomes, or ICT education. ...[T]hese studies did not look at teaching approaches that are grounded in the sound pedagogy which informs educational research."[71]

The how-to articles are replete with examples of surface and mechanistic approaches to teaching information literacy. But literacy is a complex process that goes much deeper than the simple ability to recognize and read words. True literacy opens up worlds of possibility and provides the student with the opportunity to interact in a much more meaningful way. Mechanistic approaches to learning limit the ability of students to critically engage with their world and failure to recognize its complexity leads to mechanistic and surface teaching approaches that reduce literacy "to the mechanical act of 'depositing' words, syllables, and letters *into* illiterates."[72] Kopp and Olson-Kopp asserted that "library instruction functions within the banking concept of education to the extent it can be described merely as a *transfer of objects that fosters the development of skills in the service of others* (italics in original)."[73]

Another issue that arises from librarians' lack of teacher training is that they struggle with finding ways to make their instruction personally meaningful to students. They often confront the problem of students being unable to relate the information they are supposed to learn in library instruction sessions to what they may be doing in their classes or to their lives in any meaningful way which, according to Jarvis and Ausubel, limits the possibility of deep learning.[74] Many of the current methods for teaching information literacy and library instruction strip the endeavor of any meaning to students. When students do not believe the information being taught has any significance for them, they are not open to finding ways to relate it

---

71   Mokhtar, Majid, and Foo, "Information Literacy Education," 195.

72   Paulo Freire, *The Politics of Education: Culture, Power, and Liberation* (Hadley, MA: Bergin & Garvey, 1985), 8.

73   Kopp and Olson-Kopp, "Depositories of Knowledge: Library Instruction and the Development of Critical Consciousness," 56.

74   Hay, "Using Concept Maps to Measure Deep, Surface and Non-learning Outcomes."

to their existing knowledge structures.[75] So even if librarians use methods that they hope will promote discovery learning, if the student does not find the task potentially meaningful or relevant to them personally, they are not likely to experience meaningful learning. Therefore, this important subject that perfectly aligns with critical pedagogy and is the perfect vehicle for educational empowerment is being taught in such a way that it actually goes against the theories of critical pedagogues.

However, librarians who wish to teach critical information literacy have serious obstacles to overcome. Perhaps most importantly, they have to find ways and time to delve more deeply into praxis— connecting theory with their practice and reflecting on challenges and successes in the classroom. As the following chapters will show, being able to do so depends on their professional identity as both a librarian and a teacher. Understanding teaching and learning theories is a powerful method for librarians' own empowerment. The works cited in this chapter are a good starting place for those looking to develop their knowledge of critical learning theories. For a thorough exploration of the literature on critical information literacy, see Tewell's 2015 literature review.[76]

---

75   S. Ladenson, "Paradigm Shift: Utilizing Critical Feminist Pedagogy in Library Instruction," in *Critical Library Instruction: Theories and Methods*, ed. Maria T. Accardi, Emily Drabinski, and Alana Kumbier (Duluth, MN: Library Juice Press, 2010), 105-12.

76   Tewell, "A Decade of Critical Information Literacy."

WORKS CITED

Accardi, Maria T., Emily Drabinski, and Alana Kumbier, eds. *Critical Library Instruction: Theories and Methods*. Duluth, MN: Library Juice Press, 2010.

American Library Association. "Presidential Committee on Information Literacy: Final Report." 1989. http://www.ala.org/acrl/publications/whitepapers/presidential.

Apple, Michael W., Wayne Au, and Luís Armando Gandin. *The Routledge International Handbook of Critical Education*. Routledge, 2009.

Association for Experiential Education. "What Is Experiential Education?" n.d. http://www.aee.org/about/whatIsEE.

Association of College and Research Libraries. "Information Literacy and Accreditation Agencies." 2011. http://www.ala.org/acrl/issues/infolit/standards/accred/accreditation.

Babu, B. R. "Information Literacy Competency Standards and Performance Indicators: An Overview." *DESIDOC Journal of Library & Information Technology* 28, no. 2 (2008): 56–65. http://publications.drdo.gov.in/ojs/index.php/djlit/index.

Bawden, D. "Information and Digital Literacies: A Review of Concepts." *Journal of Documentation* 57, no. 2 (2001).

Brookfield, Stephen. *The Power of Critical Theory: Liberating Adult Learning and Teaching*. Jossey-Bass Higher and Adult Education Series. San Francisco, CA: Jossey-Bass, 2005.

Bruce, C. *The Seven Faces of Information Literacy*. Adelaide, Australia: Auslib Press, 1997.

Bundy, A., ed. *Australian and New Zealand Information Literacy Framework*. 2nd ed. Adelaide, Australia: Australian and New Zealand Institute for Information Literacy, 2004. http://www.literacyhub.org/documents/InfoLiteracyFramework.pdf.

Cope, J. "Information Literacy and Social Power." In *Critical Library Instruction: Theories and Methods*, edited by Maria T. Accardi, Emily Drabinski, and Alana Kumbier, 13-28. Duluth, MN: Library Juice Press, 2010.

Dewey, John. *Experience and Education*. The Kappa Delta Pi Lecture Series, no. 10. New York: Macmillan, 1938.

Eisenhower, Cathy, and Dolsy Smith. "Discipline and Indulgence." In *Writing against the Curriculum: Anti-Disciplinarity in the Writing and Cultural Studies Classroom*, edited by Randi Gray Kristensen and Ryan M Claycomb. Lanham, MD: Lexington, 2010.

Elmborg, James. "Critical Information Literacy: Implications for Instructional Practice." *Journal of Academic Librarianship* 32, no. 2 (2006): 192-99. http://www.journals.elsevier.com/the-journal-of-academic-librarianship/.

————. "Literacies Large and Small: The Case of Information Literacy." *International Journal of Learning* 11 (2004): 1235. http://ir.uiowa.edu/slis_pubs/1/.

Fenwick, Tara J. "Expanding Conceptions of Experiential Learning: A Review of the Five Contemporary Perspectives of Cognition." *Adult Education Quarterly* 50, no. 4 (August 2000): 243-72. doi:10.1177/07417130022087035.

————. "Experiential Learning: A Theoretical Critique from Five Perspectives." Information Series No. 385. Columbus, OH: ERIC Clearinghouse on Adult, Career, and Vocational Education, 2001. http://eric.ed.gov/?id=ED454418.

Ferrare, Joseph J. "Can Critical Education Research Be 'Quantitative'?" In *The Routledge International Handbook of Critical Education*, edited by Michael W. Apple, Wayne Au, and Luis Armando Gandin, 465-82. New York: Routledge, 2009.

Foucault, Michel, and Colin Gordon. *Power/knowledge: Selected Interviews and Other Writings, 1972-1977*. New York: Pantheon, 1980.

Freire, Paulo. *Pedagogy of the Oppressed*. New rev. 20th-Anniversary ed. New York: Continuum, 1993.

————. *The Politics of Education: Culture, Power, and Liberation*. Hadley, MA: Bergin & Garvey, 1985.

Harris, B. "Encountering Values: The Place of Critical Consciousness in the Competency Standards." In *Critical Library Instruction: Theories and Methods*, edited by Maria T. Accardi, Emily Drabinski, and Alana Kumbier. Duluth, MN: Library Juice Press, 2010.

Hay, David B. "Using Concept Maps to Measure Deep, Surface and Non-learning Outcomes." *Studies in Higher Education* 32, no. 1 (February 2007): 39-57. doi:10.1080/03075070601099432.

Jacobs, Heidi L.M. "Posing the Wikipedia 'problem': Information Literacy and the Praxis of Problem-Posing in Library Instruction." In *Critical Library Instruction: Theories and Methods*, edited by Maria T. Accardi, Emily Drabinski, and Alana Kumbier, 179-98. Duluth, MN: Library Juice Press, 2010.

Jarvis, Peter. *Paradoxes of Learning: On Becoming an Individual in Society*. Jossey-Bass Higher and Adult Education Series. San Francisco, CA: Jossey-Bass, 1992.

Kellner, Douglas. "Toward a Critical Theory of Education." *Democracy & Nature: The International Journal of Inclusive Democracy* 9, no. 1 (March 2003). http://www.democracynature.org/.

Kopp, B.M., and K. Olson-Kopp. "Depositories of Knowledge: Library Instruction and the Development of Critical Consciousness." In *Critical Library Instruction: Theories and Methods*, edited by Maria T. Accardi, Emily Drabinski, and Alana Kumbier, 55-68. Duluth, MN: Library Juice Press, 2010.

Kos, Denis, and Sonja Špiranec. "Debating Transformative Approaches to Information Literacy Education: A Critical Look at the Transformative Learning Theory." In *Information Literacy. Lifelong Learning and Digital Citizenship in the 21st Century*, edited by Serap Kurbanoğlu, Sonja Špiranec,

Esther Grassian, Diane Mizrachi, and Ralph Catts, 427-35. Communications in Computer and Information Science 492. Springer International Publishing, 2014. http://link.springer.com/chapter/10.1007/978-3-319-14136-7_45.

Ladenson, S. "Paradigm Shift: Utilizing Critical Feminist Pedagogy in Library Instruction." In *Critical Library Instruction: Theories and Methods*, edited by Maria T. Accardi, Emily Drabinski, and Alana Kumbier, 105-12. Duluth, MN: Library Juice Press, 2010.

Leckie, Gloria J. *Information Technology in Librarianship: New Critical Approaches.* ABC-CLIO, 2009.

Li, LiLi, and Lori Lester. "Rethinking Information Literacy Instructions in the Digital Age." *International Journal of Learning* 16, no. 11 (2009): 569–77. http://ijl.cgpublisher.com/product/pub.30/prod.1994.

Limberg, L. "Three Conceptions of Information Seeking and Use." In *Exploring the Contexts of Information Behaviour*, edited by T. D. Wilson and D. K. Allen, 116-35. London: Taylor Graham, 1999.

Marcum, James W. "Rethinking Information Literacy." *Library Quarterly* 72, no. 1 (2002). http://www.press.uchicago.edu/ucp/journals/journal/lq.html.

Maughan, Patricia Davitt. "Assessing Information Literacy among Undergraduates: A Discussion of the Literature and the University of California-Berkeley Assessment Experience." *College & Research Libraries* 62, no. 1 (January 1, 2001): 71-85. http://crl.acrl.org/content/62/1/71.

Maybee, Clarence. "Undergraduate Perceptions of Information Use: The Basis for Creating User-Centered Student Information Literacy Instruction." *Journal of Academic Librarianship* 32, no. 1 (2006): 79-85. http://www.journals.elsevier.com/the-journal-of-academic-librarianship/.

Middle States Commission on Higher Education. *Developing Research & Communication Skills: Guidelines for Information*

Literacy in the Curriculum. Philadelphia, PA: Middle States Commission on Higher Education, 2003. https://www.msche. org/publications/Developing-Skills080111151714.pdf.

Mokhtar, Intan Azura, Shaheen Majid, and Schubert Foo. "Information Literacy Education: Applications of Mediated Learning and Multiple Intelligences." *Library & Information Science Research* 30, no. 3 (September 2008): 195-206. doi:10.1016/j.lisr.2007.12.004.

Novak, Joseph Donald. *Learning How to Learn*. New York: Cambridge University Press, 1984.

Peterson, E. "Problem-Based Learning as Teaching Strategy." In *Critical Library Instruction: Theories and Methods*, edited by Maria T. Accardi, Emily Drabinski, and Alana Kumbier, 71-80. Duluth, MN: Library Juice Press, 2010.

Rockman, Ilene F. *Integrating Information Literacy into the Higher Education Curriculum: Practical Models for Transformation*. Jossey-Bass Higher and Adult Education Series. San Francisco, CA: Jossey-Bass, 2004.

Saunders, Laura. "Regional Accreditation Organizations' Treatment of Information Literacy: Definitions, Collaboration, and Assessment." *Journal of Academic Librarianship* 33, no. 3 (2007): 317–26. http://www.journals.elsevier.com/the-journal-of-academic-librarianship/.

SCONUL Working Group on Information Literacy. "The SCONUL Seven Pillars of Information Literacy: Core Model for Higher Education," 2011.

Shor, Ira. "What Is Critical Literacy?" *Journal for Pedagogy, Pluralism & Practice* 4, no. 1 (1999). http://www.lesley.edu/journal-pedagogy-pluralism-practice/.

Sinkinson, C., and M. C. Lingold. "Re-Visioning the Library Seminar through a Lens of Critical Pedagogy." In *Critical Library Instruction: Theories and Methods*, edited by Maria T. Accardi, Emily Drabinski, and Alana Kumbier, 81-88. Duluth, MN: Library Juice Press, 2010.

Stevens-Long, Judith, Steven A. Schapiro, and Charles McClintock. "Passionate Scholars: Transformative Learning in Doctoral Education." *Adult Education Quarterly* 62, no. 2 (May 2012): 180–98. doi:10.1177/0741713611402046.

Stortz, Martha. "Academicism versus Professionalism in LIS Programs." *Public Services Quarterly* 8, no. 1 (2012): 86-90. doi:10.1080/15228959.2012.650565.

Taricani, E. "Influences of Concept Mapping and Learning Styles on Learning." In *Annual Proceedings of Selected Research and Development Papers*. Denver, CO, 2000.

Taylor, Edward. "Transformative Learning Theory." *New Directions in Adult and Continuing Education*, no. 119 (2008): 5-15. doi:10.1002/ace.

Tewell, Eamon. "A Decade of Critical Information Literacy: A Review of the Literature." *Communications in Information Literacy* 9, no. 1 (2015): 24-43. http://eprints.rclis.org/28163/.

Tisdell, Elizabeth J. "Critical Media Literacy and Transformative Learning Drawing on Pop Culture and Entertainment Media in Teaching for Diversity in Adult Higher Education." *Journal of Transformative Education* 6, no. 1 (January 1, 2008): 48-67. doi:10.1177/1541344608318970.

United Nations Educational, Scientific and Cultural Organization. "Education for All: Literacy for Life." Paris, France: United Nations Educational, Scientific and Cultural Organization, 2005. http://www.ungei.org/resources/index_581.html.

———. "Information Literacy," 2009. http://portal.unesco.org/ci/en/ev.php-URL_ID=27055&URL_DO=DO_TOPIC&URL_SECTION=201.html.

Veldof, Jerilyn R. *Creating the One-Shot Library Workshop: A Step-by-Step Guide*. Chicago: American Library Association, 2006.

Walter, Scott, Lori Arp, and Beth S. Woodard. "Instructional Improvement." *Reference & User Services Quarterly* 45, no. 3

(Spring 2006): 213-18. http://rusa.metapress.com/content/gl6570020747/.

Wilson, A. L., and L. Burket. "What Makes Learning Meaningful?" Atlantic City, NJ, 1989. http://eric.ed.gov/?id=ED313586.

Wink, Joan. *Critical Pedagogy: Notes from the Real World*. 2nd ed. New York: Longman, 2000.

CHAPTER 3

The Revelatory Power of CIL: How the Pioneers Found It and Its Relationship to Professional Identity

I first discovered critical pedagogy and then critical information literacy when I was working on my doctoral coursework. At that time, I was also deeply involved in an environmental education non-profit called What's Your Tree? (WYT), helping to write curriculum and run small groups dedicated to facilitating people's search for a life purpose as they worked on projects to improve the world. As I was first delving deeply into Paulo Freire and critical pedagogy, I spoke about him to a WYT friend who mentioned Myles Horton as being a really fascinating American critical pedagogue who had also done some work with Freire. Coincidentally, Horton and Freire developed their practices at similar times. While Freire was working in Brazil, Horton was working in the mountains of Tennessee with miners and then with civil rights leaders. I was interested in translations of critical pedagogy or similar theories to American life and education so I began researching Horton.

As I read about Horton's work as a co-founder and leader of the Highlander School in Tennessee, I could not stop seeing connections between his work and much of what I was doing as a librarian with students at my comprehensive state school in Texas. My students were much more educated and financially stable than his students, but they often seemed illiterate in terms of understanding information in the way they needed to for success or to contribute meaningfully in our current world. We often think that being able to read and write are the basic skills everyone needs, but Horton believed there were other basics that were possibly as important for the people he worked with. For example, being able to stage a protest and demand more from bosses were basic skills that the people he worked with felt they needed. The Highlander School, which was modeled after rural adult education schools in Denmark, also focused on literacy, but usually with a purpose that made it extra meaningful for the students. For example, Highlander organized literacy classes focused on helping Black Americans learn to read and write in order to pass the literacy tests required to register to vote. Importantly, the community (i.e. students) identified the skills they needed to learn.[1]

I began to see information literacy as one of those skills that is truly fundamental to living and working today, especially as I spoke with students about the Internet, Wikipedia, and news and academic sources, and learned how limited their understanding of the information structures that "informed" them was. Working with advanced journalism students was especially eye-opening as I discovered that the students who were hoping to become the informers for our society did not understand the way information was structured and, in particular, did not comprehend the power structures embedded within the information fabric. Through this work, my own understanding of information literacy changed. It became much more powerful, making my work more interesting, meaningful, and important to me.

The ideal of libraries as an essential institution in the pursuit of socially just societies was always deeply embedded in my professional ethos, but it was hard to see how I personally was contributing day to day with my library instruction classes, research guides, and other similar pursuits. My discovery of critical pedagogy was revelatory for me. It opened my eyes and mind and changed my practice. From there, I searched for other librarians who had made similar connections and discovered Elmborg, Swanson, Jacobs, Luke and Kapitzke, and others who were writing about and advocating for critical information literacy. Even though it is impossible to make everything you do as a librarian critically-oriented or feel ultra-meaningful to social justice,

---

1   Myles Horton, *The Myles Horton Reader: Education for Social Change* (Knoxville, TN: University of Tennessee Press, 2003).

having critical information literacy as the central theory that I try to build the rest of my practice on has made me a better, more engaged and effective librarian. It has had the same effect on many other librarians. The path to critical information literacy is often a revelation for librarians who discover it and then have it become a central tenet of their practice, sometimes becoming something akin to a spiritual belief that guides and feeds them.

This chapter will introduce the librarians I interviewed for my 2012-2013 study[2] and discuss how they found their way to critical information literacy, including looking at the theories and scholars whose work helped develop their ideas and inform their practice. Most of these librarians were not lucky enough to be exposed to the possible intersections of critical theory and library instruction or information literacy in easily accessible locations, such as at major conferences, in the workplace, in library school, or in the library literature. Like me, they found their way to critical theory or pedagogy through coursework outside of library and information science, while researching teaching and learning in previous teaching positions, or from stumbling upon it while reading literature in education, cultural studies, sociology, philosophy, English, or other disciplines with a strong critical theoretical tradition. Those that were lucky enough to venture into critical theory after the first critical information literacy scholars had begun publishing on it in the late 1990s to early 2000s felt they had either finally found their place in the library literature or were intrigued and wanted to push beyond their comfort zone in response to reading about it. Many felt they were changed as librarians because of it.

In the past ten years, critical information literacy has taken off and been the focus of conferences, blog posts, journal articles, and books. Librarians arguing for critical information literacy have taken places of leadership in the library instruction community and have been central to the support for ACRL's new Framework for Information Literacy in Higher Education. This has all happened because of the pioneering librarians (and others like them) who formed the basis for this book.

---

2   All names have been changed to protect participants' identities so they would feel comfortable openly discussing challenges, reservations, and professional and institutional constraints. Quotes have been edited for clarity.

WHAT ARE WE LEARNING IN LIBRARY SCHOOL?

Melissa graduated from library school in 2010. Prior to pursuing her MLS, she earned an MA and taught as a teaching assistant in cultural studies. The LIS program she chose offered an academic libraries focus, but it did not include an information literacy or library instruction course. "I think it's shameful," she said. "I'm realizing now that I am in this position, that so much of librarianship at every level in academic [libraries] is related to these really fundamental information literacy skills, and that just wasn't the focus of my library school."

I completed my MLS in 2004 and at the time, my program did not offer a course on teaching either. It turns out that user education or library instruction courses were not widespread in LIS programs until the late 1990s.[3] Over 50% of LIS programs offered a standalone library instruction course in 1999[4] and as of 2008, 86% offered at least one course on instruction, but of those only 15 explicitly included the term "information literacy" in the course title.[5] "Professional interest in information literacy can be traced back several decades,"[6] but most librarians still do not take any classes on teaching or learning during their MLS programs and have to learn to teach on the job and as they go. Walter, Arp, and Woodard argued that "even after thirty years of discussion and debate, teacher training is still a relatively minor part of the professional education for librarians even as it becomes an increasingly important part of their daily work."[7]

---

3   Loyd G. Mbabu, "LIS Curricula Introducing Information Literacy Courses alongside Instructional Classes," *Journal of Education for Library & Information Science* 50, no. 3 (Summer 2009): 203–10, http://jelis.org/.

4   Lynn Westbrook, "Passing the Halfway Mark: LIS Curricula Incorporating User Education Courses," *Journal of Education for Library & Information Science* 40, no. 2 (Spring 1999): 92–98, doi:10.2307/40324119.

5   Mbabu, "LIS Curricula Introducing Information Literacy Courses alongside Instructional Classes."

6   L. Bewick and S. Corrall, "Developing Librarians as Teachers: A Study of Their Pedagogical Knowledge," *Journal of Librarianship and Information Science* 42, no. 2 (2010): 99.

7   Scott Walter, Lori Arp, and Beth S. Woodard, "Instructional Improvement," *Reference & User Services Quarterly* 45, no. 3 (Spring 2006): 216, http://rusa.metapress.com/content/gl6570020747/.

Worse still, even when courses on information literacy are offered, it does not mean critical pedagogy will be included in the curriculum. As the scholarly literature on information literacy shows, little research has been done to create a theoretical base of information literacy pedagogy and the work that has been done, tends to focus on mechanistic, behavioral approaches. For example, Chris took courses on information literacy as part of his LIS graduate program in the early 2000s, but found critical theory and critical pedagogy were noticeably, and disappointingly, absent. Like many other critical librarians, he had learned about critical theory and critical pedagogy in courses prior to his LIS studies and thought "a really mechanistic, depository concept of education was predominant and a behaviorist model seemed pretty dominant in the literature [he] was reading about information literacy."[8]

A common critique my study participants had of their LIS programs was the almost total lack of critical theory. It is nowhere to be found in most library and information science courses. Like other librarians with affection for the ideas of critical theory, Melissa missed grappling with big meaningful ideas when she first began working as a librarian and sought ways to incorporate cultural studies and critical theory into her teaching. "The more I thought about it, the more I found these connections between information literacy and those things that I really love to study like hegemony and Marxist theory," she said. After doing a lot of this work on her own, she discovered that other librarians were also thinking and writing about using critical theory to inform information literacy.

Melissa is not alone. Only one librarian that I interviewed remembered learning about any kind of critical theory in his LIS program and that was mostly focused on the general social justice role of libraries. In his book *Critical Journeys*, Robert Schroeder[9]

---

8   Behaviorists are skills-focused, concentrating "on the measurable, overt activity of the learner" by breaking down learning objectives into tasks that are taught by giving information to the student. In contrast, critical theorists are interested in emancipating individuals from any circumstances of domination or oppression and critically oriented educators "attempt to understand processes in education in relation to their cultural, economic and political context." Critical educators' values about and approach to education is on the opposite end of the learning theory spectrum from behaviorism.

9   Robert Schroeder author, *Critical Journeys : How 14 Librarians Came to Embrace Critical Practice* (Sacramento, CA: Library Juice Press, 2014).

interviewed fourteen librarians about how they became interested in critical librarianship. His findings paralleled mine in that his interview subjects also discussed the lack of critical theory in LIS programs, with many first discovering it in courses outside LIS. A little over half of the librarians I interviewed were exposed to various critical theories in other disciplines, including cultural studies, Latin American studies, history, English, composition studies, and education. Table 2 summarizes the additional graduate degrees, and prior teaching experiences of the study participants.

2ND MASTER'S	PhD	PRIOR TEACHING
English / Creative Writing / Composition – 7 (36.8%)	English – 3 (15.8%)[2]	Grad student (semester-long courses) – 5 (26.3%)
Spanish and French – 1 (5.3%)*	LIS – 3 (15.8%)[1]	Faculty member – 1 (5.3%)
Cultural Studies – 1 (5.3%)		K-12 – 1 (5.3%)
Latino Studies (ABT) – 1 (5.3%) Philosophy – 1 (5.3%)[1]		
Total = 11 (57.9%)	Total = 6 (31.6%)	Total = 7 (36.8%)

*no critical theory in coursework; [1]after MLS; [2]before MLS

Table 2: Summary of Participants' Educational Backgrounds and Prior Teaching Experiences

ACTING ON THEORY: DISCOVERING CRITICAL INFORMATION LITERACY

The librarians I interviewed found their exposure to critical theories—whether before or after becoming a librarian—spurred them to want to find ways to incorporate critical approaches and ideas in their library work. Those that learned about it prior to beginning library careers explained that they enjoyed studying critical theories or teaching with critical pedagogy and they missed thinking about problems through a critical theoretical lens. Those that learned about it as librarians were intrigued by critical pedagogy and immediately began exploring how they could use it to teach information literacy. Whether they were desperately seeking something or just happened to stumble across it, when these librarians found their first article about critical information, they had enough of a reaction to actually change something about their practice. Learning about critical information literacy moved them to action.

Andrea had previous experience teaching critical literacy in composition courses and was already using it to inform her information literacy instruction when she discovered James Elmborg's "Critical Information Literacy: Implications for Instructional Practice." Elmborg urged librarians to reexamine how they think about information literacy and to develop a theoretically informed critical practice of librarianship in general, and information literacy in particular. He made the case for critical information literacy by problematizing dominant information literacy definitions, standards, and pedagogies and presented the alternative approach of viewing academic discourses, knowledge, and information through a critical literacy lens.[10] Andrea stated:

> Early on, I stumbled upon James Elmborg's fantastic article, which really solidified a lot of things that I'd been thinking about...it was really a lovely way for me to connect what I had known with what I was doing. I hadn't actually heard of critical information literacy until I read his article.

About half of the librarians I spoke with were not exposed to critical theories in any type of coursework. One of these, William, developed an interest in critical pedagogy on his own, at least in part from reading education journals for his liaison work. Even though he had read about it extensively, he did not try to use the ideas in his teaching until discovering the same Elmborg article that inspired Andrea. He said it was "like this light went off that I could apply these critical education ideas that I'd been thinking about forever, but just not seeming to apply it, not even thinking to apply it to my work as a librarian." As a language librarian, Shari was interested in finding

---

10   James Elmborg, "Critical Information Literacy: Implications for Instructional Practice," *Journal of Academic Librarianship* 32, no. 2 (2006): 192–99, http://www. journals.elsevier.com/the-journal-of-academic-librarianship/.

ways to bring a cultural information literacy approach to her classes with the Spanish department, but she had not learned any ways of doing so or anything about critical theory in her coursework. So she asked a colleague for article recommendations, who suggested an article by Luke and Kapitzke,[11] which is another favorite of critical librarians. Shari said that she "was just blown away" by the article and "started reading as much as I could."

Four critical information literacy publications and their respective authors and one scholar stood out as being the most influential to the librarians I interviewed. All of the authors in the top five were spoken of as scholars whose influence stretched beyond one piece. These scholars are also highly cited in the critical information literacy literature. When searching for "critical information literacy" in Google Scholar and ProQuest Research Library, Elmborg jumps to the top of the list as the most cited scholar. The top five favorites of my participants, their most influential publications, the percentage of participants that specifically mentioned each, and their number of citations as listed in Google Scholar and Web of Science are listed in Table 3 below.

Scholar	Title	Journal / Book	Participants	WoS	Google Scholar
James Elmborg	"Critical Information Literacy Implications for Instructional Practice"[1]	Journal	50%	76	279
Troy Swanson	"A Radical Step: Implementing a Critical Information Literacy Model"[2]	Journal	33.3%	13	74
Maria Accardi, Emily Drabinski, and Alana Kumbier	Critical Library Instruction: Theories and Methods[3]	Book	27.8%	13	41
Allan Luke and Cushla Kapitzke	"Literacies and Libraries: Archives and Cybraries"[4]	Journal	22.2%	12	70
Heidi Jacobs	No specific articles identified		22.2%	27	185+[5]

Table 3: Most Influential CIL Scholars and Publications

---

11   Allan Luke and Cushla Kapitzke, "Literacies and Libraries: Archives and Cybraries," *Curriculum Studies* 7, no. 3 (1999): 467–91, doi:10.1080/14681369900200066.

The Revelation of Critical Information Literacy and Professional Identity

Librarians describe the discovery of critical information literacy as something of a revelation that fills their desire to find more meaning in their work, becoming a major source of motivation and inspiration. As Shari said, "it really drives me every day...[I]nformation literacy and critical information literacy by implication seem to be the only future that libraries can have. And that's really exciting to me." When Matthew was asked how he became interested in critical information literacy, he replied "the short answer is, to maintain my sanity." Joe explained the importance of critical information to his professional identity: "For me I think it's the only thing really that makes things worth doing...if it matters to you, you don't really have a choice not to do it." Lily elaborated on this idea further:

> To me it's this great match and it's also the thing that I was looking for even though I didn't know it...So it kind of is the thing that just turned everything upside down for me. It made a huge mess, but also it really allowed me to question what I was doing and to continue to question it...It's that thing that was missing before. It's that philosophy that I just never had or I didn't know to have. And I think when you're teaching, you need that. You need that thing that grounds you, but that also inspires you. So that's what it's been for me. It's just been so valuable.

Joe argued that there was a personal religion-like element to critical information literacy and that,

> In a professional sense, it's something you believe. And it has its associated rituals and practices and a certain sort of salvation you hope for from it. But it becomes evangelical too if you don't watch it. It becomes a part of your belief system and you have to find a way to make it part of what you do every day. When I started my high school teaching job I had rooms full of failures. I was a young guy at that point and I could coach sports and I could handle a room full of rowdy boys so I taught all the struggling writers and

71

you know it would have been a really easy thing to do to just give them all Ds and get them out of there, but you could see they weren't dumb. You could see there was something in them that if you could figure out how to get to it, you could help them have better lives. And I think that's true no matter who you're working with and I think it's true in the library. I think when the reference desk is what you get, then you do that at the reference desk.

Others also talked about critical information literacy in a similar manner, as something they believed in and tried to keep present in their work, even if it was not something they could enact every day in ways they may want to. Jane asserted that "having a habit of mind" about critical information literacy changed how she talked about information even though she did not regularly use many critical pedagogical techniques because of the many institutional constraints that can get in the way of practicing critical information literacy. Chris also felt that while there was a disconnect in his "day-to-day practice between some of the more theoretical work that [he was] interested in," studying and thinking about, critical information literacy provided him with a "theoretical framework...[and] as a result, some of this work on the margin has influenced the way that I practice." So even when librarians are not able to find ways to overtly incorporate critical information literacy into their classes, many feel that believing in its importance and keeping it present in their minds still affects their practice in positive ways.

According to Kincheloe, "the recognition of [the] political complications of schooling is a first step for critical pedagogy influenced educators in developing a social activist teacher persona. As teachers gain these insights, they understand that cultural, race, class, and gender forces have shaped all elements of the pedagogical act."[12] Some critical librarians experience this type of recognition in relation to their information literacy practice by seeing at some point that cultural and sociopolitical issues impact how and what they teach and are intricately intertwined in all aspects of information literacy. Further, recognizing that they can make contributions to social justice is affirming and can provide a new direction for

---

12   Joe L Kincheloe, *Critical Pedagogy Primer* (New York: P. Lang, 2004), 2.

librarians who want to better align their practice with their values. For example, as the liaison to the education department, William had been "interested in issues of freedom and oppression,... politics and philosophy...and the role that education plays in all of that." He read the work of education scholars and radical educators, such as Freire, Ivan Illich, Paul Goodman, Emma Goldman, and others for several years without applying those ideas to his work as a librarian. When he finally made the connection that he could teach information literacy using a critical theoretical approach, it renewed him:

> I was actually at a point where I was getting just really frustrated with these little one-off instructional sessions and really questioning what it was that I was doing and the role that I was playing. And...being able to bring in everything else that I was interested in and apply it to the practice of librarianship just made so much sense and it reinvigorated me.

Daniel made similar connections between class issues and teaching information literacy after learning about critical pedagogy. As he read more about it, he:

> started to recognize some of the power dynamics at work behind how the information world is structured...[by] recognizing that certain voices seemed to be privileged over other voices—sometimes for better sometimes for worse. And how did students make those recognitions? How were faculty members talking about information sources when they often equated all sources either—like Google was bad, published sources were good, or open web was bad, published sources were good? And what kinds of conversations were we having [about that]?

He thought this was especially powerful in the context of the community college where he worked with its mission of educating often underprepared and economically disadvantaged students. Daniel credited a graduate education course that introduced him to critical pedagogy with "really open[ing] up my mind to what education could be and should be" and made him really reflect on two important questions that critical librarians working in academic libraries should be concerned with: first, what is the meaning behind the journals, books, websites, databases, and other materials purchased, collected, and/or pushed out to students?; and second, what is and what should the role of librarians be in the classroom?

Jacobs and Berg urge librarians to address these questions by aligning information literacy work with the American Library Association's *Core Values of Librarianship* to "remind librarians of the social and political dimensions of information literacy."[13] In addition to including values related to contributing to democracy, diversity, the public good, and lifelong learning, ALA has broad social responsibilities and is dedicated to informing and teaching people about critical societal problems in order to ultimately help solve them. Jacobs and Berg assert that librarians can meet this responsibility by approaching information literacy as a problem to work on together rather than as a problem to be solved. They argue that by "position[ing] ourselves and our students as critical co-investigators in the problem-posing education of information literacy, we begin to move toward a critical information literacy praxis where we can work toward the ideals of critical literacy [...] and the ideals articulated in the Alexandria Proclamation."[14]

CONCLUSION: CONFRONTING STEREOTYPES TO MAKE LIBRARIANSHIP MORE MEANINGFUL

Take a moment to think about what drew you to librarianship. Did you think the work sounded interesting? Meaningful? Like a good fit with your values? Did you want to work with people? If you answered yes to most of these, then your reasons for choosing to become a librarian match with the majority of your professional colleagues. Conversely, the primary reasons people leave the profession are because they want to pursue opportunities with more possibilities for career development and growth and "more challenging and interesting

---

13   Heidi L. M. Jacobs and Selinda Berg, "Reconnecting Information Literacy Policy with the Core Values of Librarianship," *Library Trends* 60, no. 2 (FAL 2011): 385.

14   Ibid., 390.

projects."[15] In fact, when I interviewed Eva, she was in the process of leaving librarianship to pursue a career that she hoped would be more meaningful, challenging, and personally empowering and fulfilling.

Librarian stereotypes are often blamed for the difficulties we face when trying to be seen as an important and meaningful part of the educational process. How faculty, students, and administrators view us impacts our ability to stretch beyond what has traditionally been expected of us. A major reason librarians are drawn to critical information literacy is because they are in search of ways to make their work more meaningful and more in line with the values that drew them to librarianship in the first place. But again, librarian stereotypes can stand in their way when they try to expand, change, or improve their teaching. Not only do they have to deal with the stereotypes others hold, but they also have to avoid allowing others' perceptions and expectations to define how they see themselves. Gonzalez-Smith, Swanson, and Tanaka observed that to be successful in a profession, one must "assimilate the characteristics, values, and norms of the profession."[16] Unfortunately, academic librarians are working in a profession and in broader organizations that are rife with systemic structural inequities.

As a historically feminized profession, librarianship has suffered from much lower status and pay than professions requiring comparable or less education and experience upon entry. Bayless wrote of her first impressions of librarianship in 1977 that "one thing that immediately struck [her was] the total lack of power and self-respect

---

15 Barbara B. Moran, et al., "What Today's Academic Librarians Can Tell Us about Recruiting and Retaining the Library Workforce of Tomorrow: Lessons Learned from the WILIS 1 Study," in *ACRL Fourteenth National Conference*, 2009, 335, https://www.researchgate.net/profile/Paul_Solomon2/publication/238710346_What_Today%27s_Academic_Librarians_Can_Tell_Us_About_Recruiting_and_Retaining_the_Library_Workforce_of_Tomorrow_Lessons_Learned_from_the_WILIS_1_Study/links/02e7e52cdcf04254f3000000.pdf.

16 Isabel Gonzalez-Smith, Juleah Swanson, and Azusa Tanaka, "Unpacking Identity: Racial, Ethnic, and Professional Identity and Academic Librarians of Color," in *The Librarian Stereotype: Deconstructing Perceptions and Presentations of Information Work*, ed. Nicole Pagowsky and Miriam Rigby (Chicago: Association of College and Research Libraries, 2014), 157.

as a profession."[17] Keer and Carlos argued that "as societal roles for women and other marginalized groups have changed, librarianship has also changed, but at a much more conservative pace," and "the most effective way to combat the negative effects of librarian stereotypes is to work diligently toward social justice for marginalized groups."[18] Critical librarians are invested in the broad project of social justice and believe their professional work should improve their students' lives and society. Unfortunately, how librarians are taught to teach and how the profession conceptualizes, approaches, and institutionalizes teaching are out of line with our professional values.

---

17 As cited in Gretchen Keer and Andrew Carlos, "The Stereotype Stereotype: Our Obsession with Librarian Representation," in *The Librarian Stereotype : Deconstructing Perceptions and Presentations of Information Work*, ed. Nicole Pagowsky and Miriam Rigby (Chicago: Association of College and Research Libraries, 2014), 74.

18 Ibid., 78-79.

WORKS CITED

Accardi, Maria T., Emily Drabinski, and Alana Kumbier, eds. *Critical Library Instruction: Theories and Methods.* Duluth, MN: Library Juice Press, 2010.

Bewick, L., and S. Corrall. "Developing Librarians as Teachers: A Study of Their Pedagogical Knowledge." *Journal of Librarianship and Information Science* 42, no. 2 (2010).

Elmborg, James. "Critical Information Literacy: Implications for Instructional Practice." *Journal of Academic Librarianship* 32, no. 2 (2006): 192–99. http://www.journals.elsevier.com/the-journal-of-academic-librarianship/.

Gonzalez-Smith, Isabel, Juleah Swanson, and Azusa Tanaka. "Unpacking Identity: Racial, Ethnic, and Professional Identity and Academic Librarians of Color." In *The Librarian Stereotype : Deconstructing Perceptions and Presentations of Information Work*, edited by Nicole Pagowsky and Miriam Rigby. Chicago: Association of College and Research Libraries, 2014. Horton, Myles. *The Myles Horton Reader: Education for Social Change.* Knoxville, TN: University of Tennessee Press, 2003.

Jacobs, Heidi L.M. "Information Literacy and Reflective Pedagogical Praxis." *The Journal of Academic Librarianship* 34, no. 3 (2008): 256-62. http://www.journals.elsevier.com/the-journal-of-academic-librarianship/.

———. "Posing the Wikipedia 'Problem': Information Literacy and the Praxis of Problem-Posing in Library Instruction." In *Critical Library Instruction: Theories and Methods*, edited by Maria T. Accardi, Emily Drabinski, and Alana Kumbier, 179-98. Duluth, MN: Library Juice Press, 2010.

Jacobs, Heidi L. M., and Selinda Berg. "Reconnecting Information Literacy Policy with the Core Values of Librarianship." *Library Trends* 60, no. 2 (FAL 2011): 383-94.

Keer, Gretchen, and Andrew Carlos. "The Stereotype Stereotype: Our Obsession with Librarian Representation." In *The Librarian Stereotype: Deconstructing Perceptions and Presentations of Information Work*, edited by Nicole Pagowsky and Miriam Rigby. Chicago: Association of College and Research Libraries, 2014.

Kincheloe, Joe L. *Critical Pedagogy Primer*. New York: P. Lang, 2004.

Luke, Allan, and Cushla Kapitzke. "Literacies and Libraries: Archives and Cybraries." *Curriculum Studies* 7, no. 3 (1999): 467-91. doi:10.1080/14681369900200066.

Mbabu, Loyd G. "LIS Curricula Introducing Information Literacy Courses alongside Instructional Classes." *Journal of Education for Library & Information Science* 50, no. 3 (Summer 2009): 203-10. http://jelis.org/.

Moran, Barbara B., Paul Solomon, Joanne Gard Marshall, and Susan Rathbun-Grubb. "What Today's Academic Librarians Can Tell Us about Recruiting and Retaining the Library Workforce of Tomorrow: Lessons Learned from the WILIS 1 Study." In *ACRL Fourteenth National Conference*, 2009. https://www.researchgate. net/profile/Paul_Solomon2/publication/238710346_What_ Today%27s_Academic_Librarians_Can_Tell_Us_About_ Recruiting_and_Retaining_the_Library_Workforce_of_ Tomorrow_Lessons_Learned_from_the_WILIS_1_Study/ links/02e7e52cdcf04254f3000000.pdf.

Schroeder, Robert. *Critical Journeys: How 14 Librarians Came to Embrace Critical Practice*. Sacramento, CA: Library Juice Press, 2014.

Swanson, Troy A. "A Radical Step: Implementing a Critical Information Literacy Model." *portal: Libraries and the Academy* 4, no. 2 (2004): 259-73. http://muse.jhu.edu/journals/portal_ libraries_and_the_academy.

Walter, Scott, Lori Arp, and Beth S. Woodard. "Instructional Improvement." *Reference & User Services Quarterly* 45, no. 3 (Spring 2006): 213-18. http://rusa.metapress.com/content/ gl6570020747/.

Westbrook, Lynn. "Passing the Halfway Mark: LIS Curricula Incorporating User Education Courses." *Journal of Education for Library & Information Science* 40, no. 2 (Spring 1999): 92-98. doi:10.2307/40324119.

CHAPTER 4

HOW CRITICAL LIBRARIANS TEACH: METHODS IN CONTEXT

Some of the major challenges critical librarians have raised with critical pedagogy stem from figuring out how it relates to the privileged students they work with and within their institutional contexts. In response to his popularity among American educators, Paulo Freire warned them to reinterpret or reinvent his pedagogy for their situation. Freire asserted that "to read is to rewrite" and critical pedagogues must "rewrite and recreate my ideas."[1] Critical pedagogy is not a static method of teaching, and likewise neither is critical information literacy. A central component of critical pedagogy is "a belief in the inventive potential of human beings in relationship to name and rename their shared experiences."[2] Teachers involved with the project of remaking critical pedagogy—or information literacy—for their context should consider the students they are working with and then remake their pedagogy *with* those students through dialogue and reflection.

Understanding context is important to teaching critical information literacy because it situates the teacher and student in the classroom, institution, and society. Similarly, it is important to

---

1   Kate Ronald and Hephzibah Roskelly, "Untested Feasibility: Imagining the Pragmatic Possibility of Paulo Freire," *College English* 63, no. 5 (2001): 612, doi:10.2307/379047.

2   John Pell and William Duffy, "Freire in the Agora: Critical Pedagogy and Civil Discourse," *Literacy in Composition Studies* 3, no. 1 (2015): 100, http://www.licsjournal.org/OJS/index.php/LiCS/article/viewFile/68/90.

situate information literacy work in its institutional context because it impacts how librarians envision and approach their practice, their teaching methods and content, and perceived limitations and opportunities for their work. This chapter will provide an overview of the different contexts in which critical librarians work and then a detailed description of the teaching methods that dominate critical information literacy practice, including how students respond to these types of sessions. I will end the chapter with some critiques of critical pedagogy for information literacy and begin to differentiate the difference between methods and content.

INFORMATION LITERACY MODELS AND INSTRUCTION FORMATS

The most common type of teaching by academic librarians is the one-shot instruction session. One survey of librarians from a variety of institutional types found that 94% of teaching librarians teach one-shots.[3] Another study found that 96.9% of academic libraries surveyed taught one-shots and 36.9% offered for-credit information literacy courses.[4] All of the librarians in my study taught one-shots and 31.6% taught for-credit information literacy courses.

The library literature refers to one-shot sessions as the "traditional" method of teaching information literacy[5] and "the norm for library research sessions on the majority of campuses."[6] One-shots are the main type of teaching that most librarians do, but

---

3   Sue F. Phelps, Heidi E. K. Senior, and Karen R. Diller, "Learning from Each Other: A Report on Information Literacy Programs at Orbis Cascade Alliance Libraries," *Collaborative Librarianship* 3, no. 3 (2011): 140–53, http://collaborativelibrarianship. org/index.php/jocl.

4   Erin L. Davis, Kacy Lundstrom, and Pamela N. Martin, "Librarian Perceptions and Information Literacy Instruction Models," *Reference Services Review* 39, no. 4 (2011): 686-702, doi:10.1108/00907321111186695.

5   Heidi L.M. Jacobs and Dale Jacobs, "Transforming the One-Shot Library Session into Pedagogical Collaboration," *Reference & User Services Quarterly* 49, no. 1 (2009): 72-82, http://rusa.metapress.com/index.

6   Ellysa Stern Cahoy and Robert Schroeder, "Embedding Affective Learning Outcomes in Library Instruction," *Communications in Information Literacy* 6, no. 1 (2012): 78, http://www.comminfolit.org/index.php?journal=cil.

many are also invited by the professor to teach two to three sessions for the same class. A small percentage of colleges require all students to take a semester-long information literacy course; other colleges offer elective for-credit information literacy courses, typically as part of the school's first year programming or as a general graduate course.

Information literacy programs tend to follow one of three basic models: a first year program model, the liaison model, or a combination first year and liaison model. These models describe how information literacy is implemented at an institutional level and largely define how instruction librarians' daily work is distributed, how much freedom they tend to have in the classroom, and the level of students they are likely to work with the most.

First Year Program Model

The first year program model puts first year programs in the center of an institution's information literacy strategy. These programs are typically part of first year composition classes or interdisciplinary first or second year seminars that are required core courses for all undergraduate students. Librarians working mostly within a first year program tend to teach more basic and general content, teach more sessions, and work with adjunct faculty and teaching assistants more than with full-time, permanent faculty. They often have a bit more freedom to try new things because the instructors they work with tend to be less prescriptive about what they expect the librarian to do with their classes.

Most of the librarians I interviewed described their participation in these courses as being "embedded" or a "required component." But even when one or more library instruction sessions are required, it is often up to the primary course instructor, not the librarian, to decide how involved the librarian can be and in many cases even make the major decisions about the content the librarian is allowed to teach, either by explicitly directing the librarian to teach certain concepts or demonstrate specific databases or indirectly through research assignments. Sometimes, librarians are invited by faculty to discuss and help design research assignments in order to improve the effectiveness of assignments and to ensure they mesh well with library resources. This is typically done by individual faculty members on a case-by-case basis, although there are some examples of program-wide collaborations between librarians and faculty.[7]

In addition to one-shot sessions, some of the librarians I interviewed taught semester-long courses. Some of these courses were provided through the library, which means that the course was created and proposed by the library to the curriculum committee for the college or university. After approval, all sections of the course were taught by librarians and the course designation was under the library. Melissa, Matthew, and Henry taught semester-long information literacy courses to undergraduates as part of their university's first-year programming. Melissa and Henry's courses were ongoing and not required for all students, while Matthew's had recently been cancelled, but was required for all students. These semester-long courses were typically the cornerstone of a library's first year programming for information literacy.

LIAISON MODEL

The liaison model is another common information literacy approach. In this model, librarians are assigned academic departments to work directly with. Liaison duties generally include providing library instruction, reference, and collection development services tailored for an academic department. For some librarians, especially in larger institutions, their liaison work may constitute the majority of their daily work and they may be responsible for being the primary point of contact for hundreds or thousands of students and faculty in two to four departments. For librarians in smaller institutions, liaison work may be just part of their daily duties while they are also responsible for other administrative or operational functions of the library, or they may be the liaison to several departments, freeing up other librarians in the institution to handle the operational tasks of the library.

Librarians who do most of their teaching as part of their liaison duties tend to teach fewer sessions, have to do more outreach to faculty to get classes in the library, work with more full-time, permanent

---

7   For program examples, see "Information Literacy Best Practices: Exemplary Programs," Association of College & Research Libraries (ACRL), accessed February 1, 2016, http://www.ala.org/acrl/aboutacrl/directoryofleadership/sections/is/iswebsite/projpubs/bestpractices-exemplary#collaboration.

faculty, and often have less freedom in the classroom to try new things because they have to negotiate more with faculty regarding instructional content. In some libraries, the liaison model drives the whole instruction program and liaison work is more central than first year programming.

COMBINATION MODEL

The least common approach is the combination model, in which the information literacy program is not centered around the library's liaison program or first year programs. Instead, there is a fairly even balance between the two. These programs have robust first year programs and active liaison components, and both are major sources of instruction activity for the library.

All but two of the librarians I interviewed worked in libraries that had some kind of coordinated information literacy program and roughly half worked in institutions that had information literacy goals or outcomes as part of the university requirements for all students. How information literacy is implemented when it is a university requirement is different across institutions. For some, it is specifically included as part of the general education requirements or as a mandatory component in a first or second year class that all students have to take. In any case, the information literacy program implemented by the library was closely tied to how the college or university as a whole framed information literacy. See Table 4 for a breakdown of each participant's organizational type, information literacy model, and format of courses they taught.

Participant	Model	Institution	One-shots	Multiple sessions	For-credit course
Hope	First Year	Comp	Y	N	Y
Shari	Liaison	RU	Y	Y	N
Matthew	First Year	Comp	Y	N	Y
Chris	First Year	Comp	Y	Y	N
Melissa	First Year	Comp	Y	Y	Y
Anna		RU	Y	N	N
Lily	First Year	RU	Y	N	N
Jane	First Year	Comp	Y	N	N
Eva	First Year	RU	Y	Y	N
Joe	First Year	Comp	Y	N	Y
Michael	Combination	Comp	Y	Y	Y
Chloe	Liaison	RU	Y	N	Y
Andrea	Liaison	RU	Y	N	N
Kate	Combination	4 year	Y	N	N
William	Liaison	4 year	Y	N	N
Henry	Combination	RU	Y	N	Y
Linda	Liaison	4 year	Y	N	Y
Jack	First Year	RU	Y	Y	N
Daniel	First Year	2 year	Y	N	N

Table 4: Participants' Institutional Type, IL Model, and Instructional Formats Taught

Teaching Approaches

Librarians typically use one of three approaches to teach critical information literacy: creating a student-centered learning environment, dialogue, and problem-posing methods. As standard practices in critical pedagogy classrooms, these methods are closely intertwined with, and in many cases depend upon one another, making it often difficult to tease the threads of each apart in descriptions of classroom practice. In fact, Freire often treats them as inseparable in his work. But because each element is considered necessary to constitute a truly liberatory practice, it is useful to deconstruct teachers' class descriptions to look at each element alone in order to develop a fuller understanding of the possibilities and limits of critical pedagogical praxis in the context of information literacy practice.

Student-Centered

Most of the librarians I interviewed tried to create classroom environments that were student-centered in some way. Over half prioritized a student-centered environment when developing the structure of their classes. How this environment was actually created varied and tended to depend on either how they identified as a teacher or what they hoped students would get out of the class.

Hope said that she sees critical information literacy as being "a very student-centered approach where student voice is privileged and where the authority of the teacher is sort of decentralized." Her identity as a teacher heavily influenced how she structured her classes. She believed her role was not to present herself as an "ultimate authority," but to give students a chance to have a voice and an active role in creating their own experience. She pointed out that she does this while also having learning outcomes that students accomplished. Hope described her position in the class as peer-like, which "creates an interesting dynamic in the classroom... It gets people actually physically moving around the room. And I feel like it accomplishes my objectives...so this is a method of achieving the outcomes in a way that I can feel comfortable with and feel like I'm doing something that actually makes a difference in a student's learning experience."

Jack also spoke to the importance of librarians removing themselves from a position of authority. He asserted that he was more effective with students when he positioned himself as someone "without expertise." He taught his classes from a place of non-authority and non-expertise and chose instead to focus on helping students see how research is done by researchers from the perspective of observer or translator. Lily removed herself from the position of authority by "making my classroom so constructivist that I'm barely even there. So that the students are really responsible for everything that happens in terms of the direction of the lesson, the things that we focus on, what we talk about, what they need to know and what they want to know."

Removing oneself from the position of authority can often be messy as neither learning nor research are linear processes following a set pattern. To avoid that messiness, librarians often create very contrived research demonstrations using "canned," or predetermined, search terms that bring up the results they know they want to show. While this may be useful for illustrating various features in a specific database, it presents an inaccurate picture of what the research process is like and does not create space for critical analysis or experiential learning experiences. But many librarians are fearful of losing control in the classroom and want to keep the teaching environment very neat and contained. Michael was empathetic about this challenge for some colleagues who he thought were already uncomfortable with being teachers. Adding the risks involved with pedagogy that he said puts "more power in the hands of students" can be frightening. However, as hooks pointed out, "fear of losing control shapes and informs the professorial pedagogical process to the extent that it acts as a barrier preventing constructive grappling with issues."[8]

Matthew had used canned searches as standard practice in his instruction until recently when, after reflecting on the research process, he decided that to be a more authentic teacher of the process, he needed to approach searching as the students would. He advocated for a more authentic approach when he explained an especially powerful moment from the first time he used a non-tested search in a biology class. After getting no results for *cancer* or *oncology* in Bio One, Matthew and his students finally had success with a search for *tumors*. Biologists study the biology of tumors, not the process of cancer, so their research literature uses the term tumor and must be searched accordingly, which "flabbergasted" the professor and surprised Matthew, spurring him to swear off the canned search method for good. He came to realize that using a fixed approach that did not leave room for experimentation and exploration by students prevented them from learning the realities of research and kept him from co-learning with them.

Others also had goals centered around student engagement in the research process. They wanted their teaching to respond to students' existing knowledge. These librarians also often ended up removing themselves from positions of authority, but like Matthew, they conceptualized their reasons for doing so in terms of situating

---

8   bell hooks, "Confronting Class in the Classroom," in *The Critical Pedagogy Reader*, ed. Antonia Darder, Marta Baltodano, and Rodolfo D. Torres (New York: RoutledgeFalmer, 2003), 149.

students more authentically in the research process, rather than breaking down teacher-student power structures. Those who wanted to eliminate power structures in the classroom as much as possible usually ended up with a less structured class environment than those who did not talk about teacher-student relationships in that same way.

Finding out what students already know about research and then structuring the session around their wants and needs was a common method for these librarians. Chris tried to negotiate expectations with students even in one-hour sessions by opening a web form on all of the student computers prior to the session so that as they arrived, they could type what they wanted to learn in the form and submit it to him. Anna used a snowball activity where she had students write one thing they already knew about research on a piece of paper and then ball up the paper and toss it to another student. The person that caught the paper ball opened it and shared what the first student wrote. The goal of the activity was to help Anna avoid "making a lot of assumptions about what people know and don't know." Rather than doing a special activity to get at students' prior knowledge, Jackie used discussion to try to find out the existing research processes the graduate students she worked with used. She was "absolutely convinced that people come in, particularly at the graduate level, [with their] own form of information literacy," and she thought understanding that was essential to being able to teach them what would be most helpful for them in their current context.

Most participants who used student-centered approaches also wanted to engage students more in the class session and to help them see more clearly where they fit or might fit in the process of information production, dissemination, and use. The majority did this through dialogue, but some participants also used other techniques and activities. For example, Henry used the jigsaw method to guide students through discovering how different pieces of literature or texts work together. He divided the students into small groups and then gave each group a different task or question. When the class came back together, he asked a representative from each group to report what they did or learned in hopes that students would connect all of the different pieces together to form a larger understanding of a concept. "Underlying it really is the principle that knowledge is constructed," he said. Lily had the same goals as Henry, but she took a different approach. She worked with a professor to design an assignment and a class session where students created their own database with a body of literature relevant to the class. They compiled readings based on what they thought others in the class would find helpful and organized them by using hash tags and labels to enable keyword searching within the database.

A small number of participants, including Eva, asked students to prepare for the library instruction session with a small homework assignment. Eva worked in close collaboration with the teaching faculty of the first year writing program and as part of that program, she taught three or more sessions for each class. She required students to bring specific resources that related to the day's topic to class and then used them to structure the class as she taught. For example, if the class session focused on finding scholarly literature, she asked the students to bring a scholarly article on their research paper topics. About half typically ended up bringing a scholarly article and the other half showed up with a newspaper article or something printed from a website, which allowed Eva to quickly assess students' "understand[ing] about what scholarship is and what they understand about navigating sources to find it." She talked to the students about what they brought, why, how they found it, and their evaluation of the quality and scholarliness of it. She asserted that in this exercise, their answers are never wrong, stating that, "if you find a good article in Google, you didn't do anything wrong, wherever you find it, if it's good, great."

DIALOGUE OR DISCUSSION

Many librarians, including critical librarians, use discussion in their information literacy classes. However, critical librarians try to take it up a notch, making it more akin to the dialogue of critical pedagogy. Freire argued that dialogue, combined with praxis, should lead to liberation for oppressed groups because it allows them to name their world and social conditions so that they can discover and enact revolutionary actions.[9] After working with critical pedagogy with American students at an urban college, Shor reworked Freire's goals for his students. He "believed that critical consciousness is the goal

---

9   Paulo Freire, *Pedagogy of the Oppressed*, New rev. 20th-Anniversary ed (New York: Continuum, 1993).

of Freirean education in the American higher education classroom. Critical consciousness, which encompasses being aware of power relations, analyzing habits of thinking, challenging discursive and ideological formations, and taking initiative, *is developed in student-centered dialogue* that problematizes generative themes from everyday life, topical issues from society, and academic subject matter from specific disciplines."[10] This level of dialogue is what many of the librarians I interviewed and other critical instruction librarians strive for. There are major obstacles to being able to achieve this type of dialogue in library instruction classrooms, most notably the time spent with students and the student-librarian-faculty relationship.

Almost half of the librarians I interviewed centered their classes around dialogue or discussion, and for many of those, it was the chief device they used to teach critical information literacy concepts. They believed creating opportunities for discussion in classes served multiple purposes. First, it allowed them to create a class environment that was grounded in critical pedagogical praxis and it gave them an opportunity to find out more about the students' level of knowledge, understanding, and experience with information sources and structures. It also allowed the librarian to help students form a meaningful connection with the material or to find ways that they may already be personally invested in the ideas and concepts being discussed. Finally, it gave them a voice in their own learning experience, which is essential groundwork for developing critical consciousness.

Chris stressed the value of creating space for discussion, even in a class with a short time span and fairly predetermined content, because it involves students in an important conversation about the class, giving them a feeling of ownership. Melissa believed that helping students see why the work of critical information literacy is important for them on a personal level brought them more of a sense of urgency and improved their understanding of the concepts. She did this by introducing new concepts before opening up the discussion so they had time to think, internalize, and make connections before dialoging with others about it. This is essentially critical pedagogy on a micro

---

10   Jodi Jan Kaufmann, "The Practice of Dialogue in Critical Pedagogy," \iAdult Education
      Quarterly 60, no. 5 (November 1, 2010): 458, doi:10.1177/0741713610363021.
      (empahsis mine)

scale. In order to have a true dialogue, librarians have to allow time in their one-shot classes for students to think about the topic. In long-term classes, students have time to build on what they have thought and reflected on in and between previous class sessions, but this is a luxury most librarians don't enjoy. Instead, as Melissa asserted, it is important to try to "make connections between this concept and their real life [by] going back to [their] social and political milieu [and] really really pushing that these things are personally meaningful to them."

Henry also emphasized the importance of urging students to "delve deeper into the answers or the responses that they provide." He believed that dialogue helped students understand the material and it was worth taking more time to teach using dialogue because it helped students think more deeply and critically about the content and to develop stronger understandings. He tried to have an open dialogue in his sessions by clearly articulating class goals and explaining any necessary concepts up front before leading the students through a dialogue to answer more in depth questions and "then finally to try to summarize or reach a synthesis (if that seems appropriate)."

One aspect of critical information literacy that makes it a good fit for dialogue is that the types of content librarians try to address in their classrooms are not isolated facts, but rather fairly concrete and knowable objects with an obvious social and historical existence. The use of knowable objects in dialogue between teacher and student is crucial for a Freirian critical pedagogy. According to Freire, "to be an act of knowing, the adult literacy process demands among teachers and students a relationship of authentic dialogue. True dialogue unites subjects together in the cognition of a knowable object, which mediates between them."[11]

A common theme among participants was to use the knowable object Wikipedia to spur dialogue about the social construction of information. Using a source like Wikipedia to create dialogue can be powerful because it is something students have a lot of experience with, often have clear opinions about, and view as a meaningful element in their lives. Andrea used Wikipedia in a lot of her classes, especially with the history department, and was very pleased with

---

11   Paulo Freire, *The Politics of Education: Culture, Power, and Liberation* (Hadley, MA: Bergin & Garvey, 1985), 49.

how much it seemed to resonate with students. She would start with asking students to think about what was good and bad about Wikipedia to get them to think about other types of sources and their strengths and weaknesses. She said "what I really loved about talking about Wikipedia with students is they had tons of things to say." She thought that they seemed to have been trained to say Wikipedia was bad, while they secretly relied on it as an essential source, which created a huge dialogic opportunity that was so meaningful to students that they often stop her on campus to talk more about it. More examples of how participants used Wikipedia are presented and expanded on in the discussion of critical content in chapter 5.

PROBLEM-POSING

Freire argued that critical teachers committed to liberation "must abandon the goals of deposit-making and replace it with the posing of problems of human beings in relation with their world."[12] In problem-posing approaches, the student-teacher relationship is dialogic, such that each has something to contribute and receive and actual lived experiences must be integrated as part of the exploration of knowledge.[13] Because problem-posing approaches use dialogue as part of the process, they were sometimes difficult to disentangle from the use of dialogue in the participants' descriptions of their classes. Some of the other participants likely structured their dialogue as part of a problem-posing approach also, but five librarians I spoke to said they did so intentionally. Two additional participants, Melissa and Matthew, did not specifically state that they used a problem-posing approach. Instead, they used what they called a "rhetorical approach," but it included very similar techniques of looking at a problem, analyzing, and reflecting on it. Melissa explained that rhetoric in this sense meant "methods of using language to persuade."

Problem-posing approaches typically take the form of structuring the entire class session around a real world problem or constructing a problem for students to consider and base their discussions on. Anna did the former in an English class she taught to prepare the students

---

12   Freire, *Pedagogy of the Oppressed*, 60.

13   Antonia Darder, Marta Baltodano, and Rodolfo D. Torres, eds., *The Critical Pedagogy Reader* (New York: Routledge Falmer, 2003).

for a research paper that had been assigned for later in the semester. Since she was asked to teach the class the first week in the semester, the students had no research topics and had not yet engaged with any of the course content. Anna felt structuring the class around a problem would make it more meaningful and hopefully feel less abstract to the students. She presented students with the problem of having to write a paper on a post 9/11 American novel. She asked them how they would approach the assignment and then as a class, they experimented with strategies and discussed and problematized their findings, which included discussing their role in the process as information consumers.

Matthew created an assignment based on fears created or encouraged by the media for his semester-long information literacy course to get students thinking about and interested in the full implications of information literacy by engaging them in a real world problem to start the semester. He had them "pick a fear that the media perpetuated in some way. For example, [they've reported] there's bacteria on the lemons that you get in your water at restaurants." They had to do a small research assignment to find out "Is it going to kill you? Is this worth freaking out about? Is it overblown? Or is it just the right amount of fear?" This assignment is an excellent example of a problem-posing approach because it encourages students to integrate their lived experiences into their learning.

Lily followed a similar approach to Matthew by asking students to confront and analyze their role in the information construction and dissemination process. She wanted them to think about where they entered the process and in what ways they may be influenced by or even complicit in oppressive structures. Rather than structuring the class around how to find and make sense of information, she asked them to consider: "What if your role in this space is as an information consumer and creator? What should you pay attention to when you're [confronting] these voices and perspectives? How do you want to engage with and contribute to the conversations?"

While Anna, Matthew, and Lily's classes were on different topics and in support of different disciplines, they all asked similar questions of the students, which works for teaching students about information because it allows them to become the owners of their learning and find their own answers, and to see that information processes and systems are social constructions that they have a role in.

An advocate of problem-based instruction sessions, Michael argued that this approach allowed his students to "not only...construct their understanding of how information is organized [and] how to solve a problem you've posed, [it] also helped students recognize that knowledge itself is something that's constructed."

A popular misconception of critical pedagogy is that it is laissez faire or a free for all where students chart their own course and the teacher lets them go off on their own tangents or sets them free to do whatever they want. In truth, structure is a necessary component in the problem-posing classroom. "The educator's responsibility rests precisely in his or her duty to furnish the conditions for effective (by which Freire means critical, dialogical, and praxical) learning to take place."[14] This includes providing directions, structure, curriculum content, and setting the stage for academic rigor. Andrea provided an example of this:

> More and more I'm doing classes and activities and approaches that present students with a bit of a problem. So the problem might be how do you find information in your area? And we approach it as a problem, and we brainstorm on ways to do that. And I come up with activities that, I sort of know where they're going to end up, but I think it's really great for students to have these ideas themselves, and start to make these connections themselves. But if I approach it as communal: here's this issue, what are we going to do about it?—students become much more engaged with it, they become invested. And it's a much more interesting experience for me and for them, and also the prof, to be really engaged with these ideas...The more I challenge them and the more I give them real scenarios that they as historians or English majors or citizens or just general people in the world—giving them those kinds of questions really engages them, and I think makes them see that there are connections between what they are learning in class and in the library sessions and the lives that they lead and they might lead and the work they may do.

---

14   Peter Roberts, *Education, Literacy, and Humanization Exploring the Work of Paulo Freire*, Critical Studies in Education and Culture Series (Westport, CT: Bergin & Garvey, 2000), 59.

Rhetorical techniques in problem-posing

The rhetorical techniques Melissa and Matthew used to structure their problem-posing classes have support from some of the most prominent scholars working in critical information literacy.[15] Jacobs argued for following the example set by the discipline of Composition and Rhetoric to use problem-based approaches to teach literacy because, like other forms of literacy, information literacy "must be specific, relevant, meaningful, and contextualized for the particular learners and their contexts."[16] Jacobs emphasizes that there cannot be a set method, technique, or device to teach critical information literacy. She argues that engaging with, discussing, and reflecting on methods, techniques, and devices to teach information literacy is the problem that critical librarians should pose and work on as they teach students about information. Librarians have to "shift from being the 'teacher-of-the-students' to the 'teacher-student with students-teachers,'" so that we are learning with students, "becom[ing] engaged learners, delv[ing] deeply into our own problem-posing and embody[ing] the kind of engagement we want to see in our students."[17]

Both Matthew and Melissa used rhetorical techniques to teach, but also to reflect on the teaching and learning process they encountered in their classes. Matthew "developed a sort of a rhetorical approach to information literacy where the centerpiece was helping students understand how their disciplines, or even how more generally groups used information." He asserted that using the ideas of rhetoric gave him a way to explain the complicated ideas behind critical information literacy and gave the students an entry point for their discussions. It also gave him a pathway into engaging with both the students and the content so he could learn along with them, which had allowed him to improve as a teacher.

Melissa used rhetoric as a way to guide students through the process of thinking about popular media sources. She developed an exercise where students used rhetorical devices as a rubric to help them

---

15   Heidi L.M. Jacobs, "Information Literacy and Reflective Pedagogical Praxis," *The Journal of Academic Librarianship* 34, no. 3 (2008): 256-62; James Elmborg, "Literacies Large and Small: The Case of Information Literacy," *International Journal of Learning* 11 (2004): 1235.

16   Jacobs, "Information Literacy and Reflective Pedagogical Praxis," 13.

17   Ibid., 19.

evaluate media. She showed a clip of a television program that was full of persuasive language and ideology and provided students with a list of rhetorical devices to use as "a rubric for critical thinking." Then the students chose the rhetorical devices that the television program used and discussed their evaluations of the show, which provided students with "a more concrete way to think about something very abstract." She explained the purpose of the exercise and the scholars that influenced it:

> It was about examining media through what I call these pillars of media literacy; it's really through a lens of cultural studies. So we examined news and commercials, films, things like that, by using these concepts of hegemony, and ideology, as informed by Althusser and representation as informed by Stuart Hall's ideas of representation, that we make meaning by the way that something is represented.

Non-Critical Methods and Challenges to Critical Information Literacy Methods

Unfortunately critical methods do not always work in the information literacy classroom. Almost half of the librarians I spoke with stated unequivocally that they used non-critical methods in their instruction sessions either sometimes or all of the time. Many of the others implied the same. The primary reasons for not using critical methods were problems with being able to match the structure of critical information literacy methods with the current institutionally-defined structure of library instruction; lack of alignment of goals for critical information literacy and the classes and/or the professor the librarian was teaching for; and a general lack of time to accomplish any meaningful goals.

Despite reading a lot about critical information literacy and being interested in the ideas that it presents, Jane was concerned that the format for library instruction is not a good fit for critical methods because "the format of the way we structure library instruction or information literacy instruction, doesn't afford any opportunities really to do anything critical." Eva had similar thoughts about the difficulties of using critical methods to teach information literacy. She put forth the common assertion that librarians do not always have the power to control how the class is run because "we're still adjunct to a faculty member who has their own plan for what to do and their own pedagogy." She also thought the institutional context of the university got in the way of her ability to do much with critical approaches because "there's *so* many constraints."

How and what was taught in participants' information literacy sessions had to fit within the larger goals of the course the librarian was teaching for. There was often some leeway in what librarians could teach, but how this was negotiated differed, especially in relation to whether the course was a major course taught in the disciplines or a general first-year course. Goals for information literacy sessions in the disciplines were usually negotiated with the professor who teaches the course. The goals for information literacy sessions for first year programs were usually very specific and had been negotiated with the director of the overall composition or other first-year program and may or may not also include a discussion of goals and content with the instructor actually teaching the course. Participants tended to have more freedom to try different methods in first year program courses because they were less likely to be closely monitored by a full-time professor, but the learning outcomes were often much more restrictive and basic than for upper level courses in the disciplines.

Most of the sessions Jane taught were for the first year composition program and second year core seminar and she observed that instructors often have a very narrow goal for these library sessions. Students typically have an assignment that requires them "to find three papers," and her job is to "get them to find those three papers." To make sure they get what they need, she "mostly give[s] a ten or twelve minute demo and then work[s] with them one-on-one to find the three papers that they need."

Chris believed that "certain mechanistic...pieces of information are important to communicate" because many of the students he worked with were first generation students or students without a lot of preparation prior to attending college. They need to know basic information like how to find a book on the shelf, what their barcode is, and how to access their library accounts. So for him, "the goals that I might have that are more engaged kinds of things that critical information literacy is interested in frequently have to take a backseat to addressing what I would say are more basic literacies."

In all cases, librarians deferred to faculty goals for information literacy sessions, even if the professor had a limited or outdated understanding of the current information environment. Regardless of the discipline or level of class, professors often had clearly defined goals for the content they wanted students to learn, which had an obvious effect on teaching methods as well. Every librarian I interviewed talked about aligning their instructional goals with what the professor wanted them to teach. In the cases of it preventing them from being able to use critical methods, it was usually because the professor wanted them to demonstrate a specific database or other tool, show the relevant features, answer questions about the tool, and be done. While there was some amount of frustration with this, the participants were generally accepting of and resigned to this reality. Linda provided a typical response to this situation:

> I think you know that there is a time and place for doing tool-based sorts of things. If students need three articles for something, talking about bias might not be the best time to do that. Focusing on delivering the content that the faculty member needs for that particular assignment is really important.

The other big issue that got in the way of librarians' ability to use critical methods was just a general lack of time. Most library sessions are fifty minutes, which does not allow a lot of time to create a student-centered environment, make space for meaningful dialogue, or explain and work through problems.

DO CRITICAL PEDAGOGICAL METHODS WORK IN THE LIBRARY CLASSROOM?

Most of the librarians I interviewed felt students responded positively to critical information literacy and that it was an effective teaching method. When asked how students responded to critical information literacy sessions they had taught, the majority answered with phrases such as "I've had a lot of really good feedback from students," "it turned out really awesome and students loved it," "they really enjoyed it," "they seem to get it and seem interested," and "students become much more engaged." However, some had experiences when critical information literacy instruction sessions did not go well and they thought students were resistant to critical information literacy. The following paragraphs provide examples of when things went well, when they went wrong, and the participants' thoughts on why that was the case for each.

STUDENT ENGAGEMENT AND EMPOWERMENT

My study participants thought critical information literacy methods and content worked well for a variety of reasons, including that it changed the dynamic in the classroom, opened up conversations about issues they were interested in, gave students more space to think and make connections, and it was empowering. Hope enjoyed that it "lifts some of the burden from [her]" and "changes things up...[and] creates a sort of energy that this is a different kind of classroom." Several others thought it opened up conversations and gave students the freedom and voice to talk about the issues in a way that was meaningful to them and drew on their previous experiences. For example, Kate taught a class on Google where the students "ended up having an entire discussion...[for] ten or fifteen minutes...about these issues and how surprised they were."

Many participants thought critical information literacy worked well because it offered opportunities to empower students and more fully engage them in their education. Empowerment as a goal for critical information literacy works well because it is concerned with "question[ing] the social, political, and economic forces involved in the creation, transmission, reception, and use of information," and "recognizes the complicity of the individual—and the individual as a community member—in information-based power structures and struggles."[18]

Andrea felt the students she taught were already somewhat aware of these issues and that formally addressing them in class gave them a gateway into talking more deeply about it, which could be empowering because "they're not idiots, they know that they're being manipulated. But they just couldn't put a word to it. They didn't have a language

---

18   B. Harris, "Encountering Values: The Place of Critical Consciousness in the Competency Standards," in *Critical Library Instruction: Theories and Methods*, ed. Maria T. Accardi, Emily Drabinski, and Alana Kumbier (Duluth, MN: Library Juice Press, 2010), 273.

to talk about it. So I think giving them that language allowed them to be more empowered...[and] really think through what these things meant." She pointed out that this can sometimes lead to a bit of an existential crisis for students where they start to question how they can trust anything. But she reasoned that it is okay because "that's the beginning of really understanding what research is about."

Michael agreed that teaching critical information literacy could lead to transformative and empowering experiences for students if educators can "get students to make the connection between their own process of knowledge construction and knowledge construction in general," so they can potentially realize that they have the power to produce and transform knowledge. Developing curriculum where "the learning process is negotiated, requiring leadership by the teacher, and mutual teacher-student authority"[19] is a hallmark of empowering education.

In addition to wanting students to confront the wider world of information, many participants were especially focused on helping students become empowered in relation to the process of scholarship. Students often feel very separate from the work of scholars and have a difficult time seeing how it relates to them. When Eva described how she first became interested in critical pedagogy, it was largely in response to dealing with teaching freshman composition classes for the first time and trying to figure out how to enable students to see that what they were doing in their coursework related to their lives.

> I realized that the students...wouldn't understand why we were doing things in class,...and I would say 'well, thinking is important.' And then I got to the point where I realized that they didn't really understand why thinking was important. I couldn't use that as a premise for the course because they didn't necessarily buy it. And so I started using Paulo Freire's chapter from Pedagogy of the Oppressed on the banking concept of education and we would read that... and talk about what it means to have critical consciousness and what it means to learn and what the value is of thinking as a citizen. And so...later in the semester [when] we would

---

19   Ira Shor, *Empowering Education: Critical Teaching for Social Change* (University of Chicago Press, 2012), 15.

talk about why we were doing something, we could always bring it back to why does being a critical thinker play a valuable role in your life or in the life of a community. We had some grounding then.

Eva developed these ideas within the context of teaching semester-long freshman composition courses as a graduate student, but they stayed with her when she became a librarian. Other librarians also wanted students to see how their coursework had personal and societal meaning beyond the classroom walls because empowerment in critical discourses is about more than empowering individual students in the classroom. It is about looking at and confronting power relations in the wider world, including the political nature of power.[20] Many critical librarians are dedicated to helping students develop a more complete awareness of the structure of scholarly communication, including becoming cognizant of their role in it and the potential they have to make their contributions deeper and more meaningful. Lily stressed that she wanted students to "understand that they also have a contribution to make in the scholarly conversation and we... [can] encourage them and empower them to do that."

STUDENT RESISTANCE

About one-third of the librarians I spoke with described instances where students were resistant to critical information literacy methods. Hope was very positive about her experiences with using critical pedagogical approaches overall. In some ways, she seemed the most confident of all of the interviewees about what she was doing and she was the most consistent in her use of critical information literacy approaches for the majority of her classes, but even she experienced resistance when "students don't want to get up in front of the room." Her response to this type of resistance was to "make them do it anyway," even though this was the only thing she left her instruction sessions not feeling great about.

---

20   Jennifer Gore, "What We Can Do for You! What Can 'We' Do for 'You'? Struggling over Empowerment in Critical and Feminist Pedagogy," in *The Critical Pedagogy Reader*, ed. Antonia Darder, Marta Baltodano, and Rodolfo D. Torres (New York: Routledge Falmer, 2003), 331-48.

Anna also described moments of feeling resistance from the students when she asked them to participate in class discussions or exercises. She worked mostly with freshman students and found that "there is kind of this reticence to respond to questions or to share something from themselves." She attributed this, at least in part, to the testing-heavy public schools her students came from. But she was a proponent of modeling for students and professed a great love and excitement for what she was teaching. She argued that the combination of these two things and pushing students until one or two responded usually got her through that obstacle. She asserted that "students like to be heard, they want to be able to talk, and they want to...describe their experiences...[so] if you can... get a couple people in the class doing that then I think it kind of radiates outward."

Kate and Daniel felt that some students push back against critical methods because they are very practically minded and just want to know what they need for their assignment. Kate thought "they don't want to think about how to get the answers. They just want you to tell them what is right, what [they] should do." Like Anna, she thought it was possible to push through this and get students to the point where they saw how it related to them so they got more excited about the ideas, but she found their initial response was often resistance:

> I think students actually push back against it a lot...[T]he idea that they're supposed to do the work and they're supposed to do the thinking, that I'm actually presenting an image or a topic or an idea, and they're supposed to look at it and think about how they're searching, how their terminology works, why this database or not, how databases construct stuff. They don't actually want to do the thinking, particularly in the beginning, they want you to tell them use this database, use these terms—you're supposed to tell me. But usually if they get into it, particularly the upper level students, they get really excited.

Shari and Henry described experiences when students looked at them like they were "crazy." They both thought this stemmed from them not explaining to students what they wanted them to do well enough. Henry had gotten feedback from students that they "initially don't understand me because my questions are too broad and then I'll go back and clarify." Shari also thought that there were times when she may not be making her "goals clear, or it doesn't seem clear to them, or it doesn't seem too obvious, or it's too complicated."

Anna talked about a similar experience she had in the context of the upper level English course where she asked students to do research on the post 9/11 American novel. She wanted to give them a lot of room to play around with the topic and find their own way, but she did not get the outcome she hoped for from students. She thought part of the problem was that she did not provide enough guidance on what she wanted from them or did not explain it well enough, but still she thought there was some general discomfort with ambiguity on the part of the students.

Matthew felt a similar disconnect between what he was trying to accomplish with his fear assignment and the actual outcome of the assignment. He found that it was not that students could not find information; it was that "they weren't finding the good stuff" that he expected from them. He asked them to investigate how the media perpetuated a fear and to find sources that proved or disproved it. He had hoped that they would find research articles discussing the research behind the fear, but that was not what he received from students. Instead, almost all of them turned in newspaper articles. He used this exercise for six years and of the "thousand or so resources that the students provided, of the hundreds of students that completed the assignment," he estimated that only six actually turned in what he wanted to see and what he initially expected. But, he said "it gave me this idea that students had absolutely no idea or understanding of how information was organized."

Matthew used this information to guide how he taught his semester-long information literacy class and one-shot sessions. He constantly learned from students in class discussions and from how they approached assignments and used it to restructure his pedagogy. Other participants responded to pedagogical failures in the same way, in that they used it to help guide how and what they taught in the future, which is exactly what Jacobs urges librarians to do—adopt a theoretically-informed praxis that "simultaneously strives to ground theoretical ideas into practicable activities and use experiential knowledge to rethink and re-envision theoretical concepts."[21]

---

21   Jacobs, "Information Literacy and Reflective Pedagogical Praxis," 15.

CONCLUSION: CRITICAL CONTENT V. CRITICAL PEDAGOGY

Enacting critical pedagogy in the classroom can be quite hard. Enacting critical pedagogy in the *library* classroom is harder still. Some critical librarians question if it is even possible. Jane and Eva robustly critiqued critical information literacy throughout their interviews. Both were advocates of critical pedagogy, were well versed in the literature surrounding it, and were also interested in feminist pedagogy. Eva specifically discussed critiques of critical pedagogy by feminist theorists as being especially meaningful to her personally. Interestingly, both Eva and Jane spoke at length about the impossibility of enacting critical pedagogy in university settings in general and library instruction classrooms in particular. While others identified areas where they thought it was difficult and recognized clear challenges, Jane and Eva saw it as essentially impossible. They contrasted using critical pedagogical methods with teaching critical content, which they thought was far more doable because the ideas could be integrated into the general content of the class session, even if methods or techniques that would fall under the rubric of critical pedagogy were not used.

Jane felt strongly that it was important for scholars and students to critique the production, dissemination, and organization of knowledge, but was not convinced that it was possible to teach much of that to students in a library instruction class because there was prescribed content that she had to make sure students knew to complete their course assignments. She also did not think there was enough time or the proper context to use critical pedagogical methods in her classes, though she thought that it was possible to include some critical content and that "having a habit of mind about that changes the way you talk about information in the classroom."

Similarly, Eva argued that creating a critical pedagogical class environment in the university context was not possible, but that "the one place where it is more possible is if you look at it as social justice as it relates to scholarly communication and the dissemination of research and things like that...That's theoretically possible...We can teach those things and those questions." Eva formed these opinions over many years of teaching in universities, first in composition and then in the library. She had personally tried and knew many colleagues who had tried to enact critical pedagogy without success.

Eva described her "most experimental" information literacy class, which she designed for a food and social justice course with a philosophy professor. The professor was a friend of Eva's and was open to trying something new for the library portion of the course, which included three sessions. Eva pronounced the class "a total failure." The sessions were meant to be student conceived and led. Eva and the professor had the students decide what they needed to learn about research and then organize the topics into categories. The students then broke into groups and each group chose a category of the research topics that they were supposed to research and then present a mini class session on. They spent the time in the class sessions working in their groups and with Eva and the professor to accomplish these tasks.

Eva loved the concept for the class, but ultimately decided "it doesn't work because the students learn their little module or... questions they are trying to answer, but they're not teachers. And so you realize oh wait I actually know how to teach somewhat and they don't and so they end up learning only this one little thing and sitting through kind of bad presentations by the rest of the class." She thought to pull it off successfully "would have required a lot more intensive work with them."

One of my justifications for breaking critical methods apart from critical content in this book was in response to the challenges presented by Eva and Jane's critiques. Critical pedagogy in the purest sense as it was understood and enacted by Paulo Freire and his followers would be next to impossible to pull off in library classrooms. The library profession, libraries, and colleges and universities present obstacles that while not entirely insurmountable, are big enough that they heavily impact librarians' freedom in the classroom. The teaching methods that critical pedagogy offers us, combined with the rich possibility offered by critical information literacy content, provides a set of ideas and concepts that librarians can use to make their information literacy work more critical, engaging, and meaningful. But when critical methods are not possible, critical content can help librarians get closer to meeting their teaching goals. In the next chapter, I will present some ideas for critical information literacy content.

Works Cited

Cahoy, Ellysa Stern, and Robert Schroeder. "Embedding Affective Learning Outcomes in Library Instruction." *Communications in Information Literacy* 6, no. 1 (2012): 73-90. http://www.comminfolit.org/index.php?journal=cil.

Darder, Antonia, Marta Baltodano, and Rodolfo D. Torres, eds. *The Critical Pedagogy Reader*. New York: Routledge Falmer, 2003.

Davis, Erin L., Kacy Lundstrom, and Pamela N. Martin. "Librarian Perceptions and Information Literacy Instruction Models." *Reference Services Review* 39, no. 4 (2011): 686-702. doi:10.1108/00907321111186695.

Elmborg, James. "Literacies Large and Small: The Case of Information Literacy." *International Journal of Learning* 11 (2004): 1235. http://ir.uiowa.edu/slis_pubs/1/.

Freire, Paulo. *Pedagogy of the Oppressed*. New rev. 20th-Anniversary ed. New York: Continuum, 1993.

———. *The Politics of Education: Culture, Power, and Liberation.* Hadley, MA: Bergin & Garvey, 1985.

Gore, Jennifer. "What We Can Do for You! What Can 'We' Do for 'You'? Struggling over Empowerment in Critical and Feminist Pedagogy." In *The Critical Pedagogy Reader*, edited by Antonia Darder, Marta Baltodano, and Rodolfo D. Torres, 331-48. New York: Routledge Falmer, 2003.

Harris, B. "Encountering Values: The Place of Critical Consciousness in the Competency Standards." In *Critical Library Instruction: Theories and Methods*, edited by Maria T. Accardi, Emily Drabinski, and Alana Kumbier. Duluth, MN: Library Juice Press, 2010.

hooks, bell. "Confronting Class in the Classroom." In *The Critical Pedagogy Reader*, edited by Antonia Darder, Marta Baltodano, and Rodolfo D. Torres. New York: Routledge Falmer, 2003.

"Information Literacy Best Practices: Exemplary Programs | Association of College & Research Libraries (ACRL)." Accessed February 1, 2016. http://www.ala.org/acrl/aboutacrl/directoryofleadership/sections/is/iswebsite/projpubs/bestpractices-exemplary#collaboration.

Jacobs, Heidi L.M. "Information Literacy and Reflective Pedagogical Praxis." *The Journal of Academic Librarianship* 34, no. 3 (2008): 256-62. http://www.journals.elsevier.com/the-journal-of-academic-librarianship/.

Jacobs, Heidi L.M., and Dale Jacobs. "Transforming the One-Shot Library Session into Pedagogical Collaboration." *Reference & User Services Quarterly* 49, no. 1 (2009): 72-82. http://rusa.metapress.com/index.

Kaufmann, Jodi Jan. "The Practice of Dialogue in Critical Pedagogy." *Adult Education Quarterly* 60, no. 5 (November 1, 2010): 456-76. doi:10.1177/0741713610363021.

Pell, John, and William Duffy. "Freire in the Agora: Critical Pedagogy and Civil Discourse." *Literacy in Composition Studies* 3, no. 1 (2015): 95-107. http://www.licsjournal.org/OJS/indcx.php/LiCS/article/viewFile/68/90.

Phelps, Sue F., Heidi E. K. Senior, and Karen R. Diller. "Learning from Each Other: A Report on Information Literacy Programs at Orbis Cascade Alliance Libraries." *Collaborative Librarianship* 3, no. 3 (2011): 140-53. http://collaborativelibrarianship.org/index.php/jocl.

Roberts, Peter. *Education, Literacy, and Humanization Exploring the Work of Paulo Freire*. Critical Studies in Education and Culture Series. Westport, CT: Bergin & Garvey, 2000. http://site.ebrary.com/lib/reed/Top?id=10017980.

Ronald, Kate, and Hephzibah Roskelly. "Untested Feasibility: Imagining the Pragmatic Possibility of Paulo Freire." *College English* 63, no. 5 (2001): 612-32. doi:10.2307/379047.

Shor, Ira. *Empowering Education: Critical Teaching for Social Change*. Chicago: University of Chicago Press, 2012.

Chapter 5

What Critical Librarians Teach: Avoiding the Banking Concept with Critical Content

In the fall of 2014, a major Ebola outbreak in West Africa took over the news headlines. As doctors worked to control the virus, the media bombarded us with information about the dangers of Ebola and warned of a possible outbreak in the United States. Twitter blew up with alarming tweets like this one from September 30: *@CNN: #BREAKING: 1st diagnosed case of #Ebola in the U.S. confirmed*, which snowballed, causing fear to spread through the country so fast that by November, Americans ranked Ebola as their third biggest healthcare concern in a Gallup poll.[1] Emilio Ferrara, a computer scientist at the University of Southern California, tracked the spread of Ebola hysteria on Twitter, finding that the "'fear-rich' tweets...triggered re-tweets twice as fast, on average, than neutral posts or posts conveying other emotions such as happiness...Beyond the Ebola scare, he says, the snowballing of fear online likely explains why smear campaigns dominate politics, why Twitter rumors can crash the stock market, and why ISIS's beheading videos have become successful propaganda."[2]

News journalism and social media present an interesting case to consider when thinking about the complexity of the information

---

1 Lydia Saad, "Ebola Ranks Among Americans' Top Three Healthcare Concerns," Gallup.com, accessed March 4, 2016, http://www.gallup.com/poll/179429/ebola-ranks-among-americans-top-three-healthcare-concerns.aspx.

2 Len Small, "Nothing Snowballs Online Like Fear," *Nautilus*, February 18, 2016, http://nautil.us/issue/33/attraction/how-ebola-infected-twitter.

landscape. The reach of social media is indisputable[3], but as Ferrara found, the actual facts behind Tweets can easily be obscured by the hyperbole of the language used to grab people's attention. By the end of the Ebola outbreak, there were only four confirmed cases in the U.S, but "more than 1 in 6 Americans believed Ebola was the nation's biggest health problem."[4] But before swearing off Twitter, take into account the platform that social media sites have created for a more diverse set of voices to be heard. While minority Americans are still largely excluded from opportunities to control what is published and produced in mainstream books and media, new forms of media provide new opportunities. Twitter enabled the Black Lives Matter movement to gain hold in 2015 and racial controversies to dominate American cultural conversations with social media campaigns like 2016's #OscarsSoWhite.

The success of these campaigns combined with the demographics of social media use reinforce the notion that "The Cyber Left is about flattening hierarchies, flattening governance processes, combined with using the logic of social networks for deep consensus building."[5] 96% of young African American Internet users use a social networking site, and 40% of those use Twitter, which is 12% higher than their White counterparts.[6] "Meanwhile, what remains of print journalism is shifting, morphing into a loose web of digital outfits populated by a corps of underpaid young freelancers and keyboard hustlers, Twitter fiends and social-media soothsayers."[7] Those hardest hit by the shifts in traditional publishing are women, minorities, and older people. In 2015, 89% of *Publisher Weekly*'s members self-identified as White, while only 5% identified as Asian, 3% as Hispanic, 2% as mixed race,

---

3   40% of people under 35 reported using social media as their primary news source in a 2015 poll. Ibid.

4   Lydia Saad, "Ebola Ranks Among Americans' Top Three Healthcare Concerns."

5   Todd Wolfson, as cited in Elizabeth Day, "#BlackLivesMatter: The Birth of a New Civil Rights Movement," *The Guardian*, July 19, 2015, sec. World News, http://www.theguardian.com/world/2015/jul/19/blacklivesmatter-birth-civil-rights-movement.

6   Ibid.

7   Dale Maharidge, "These Journalists Dedicated Their Lives to Telling Other People's Stories. What Happens When No One Wants to Print Their Words Anymore?," *The Nation*, March 2, 2016, para. 10, http://www.thenation.com/article/these-journalists-dedicated-their-lives-to-telling-other-peoples-stories/.

and a tiny 1% as African American.[8] In February 2016, the *New York Times* compiled a list of "503 of the most powerful people in American culture, government, education, and business, and found that just 44 are minorities."[9]

These numbers illustrate why including critical content in information literacy classes is important. When we stick with only talking to students about the sources included in mainstream channels, we limit their view of the information world. White upper and middle class voices dominate more than just the creation of information, but also how it is structured, organized, and disseminated, which shows up in the language librarians and other indexers use to describe sources and in where and how easily those sources can be found. But when looking at new media types and forms of information, evaluation becomes even more critical.

In response to the complicated political, social, and economic nature of information, all of the librarians I spoke with were determined to include critical content in their classes. Opportunities to do so were minimal in some cases, but they were still resolved to find ways to work in critical content even if it was in small ways. Most taught critical source evaluation—including teaching students how knowledge is produced and disseminated and deconstructing the scholarly versus popular dichotomy of academic research—and problematized subject headings and other language used in library catalogs, databases, and the Internet in order to encourage students to think more holistically about information, such that they understand that it is part of the larger sociopolitical world that produces it.

Some of the major things critical librarians want students to learn are: developing understandings about research not being linear; that all information is part of the sociopolitical world; and the research process is complex and more important than their previous educational experiences may imply. They want students to learn more

---

8   Jim Milliot, "The PW Publishing Industry Salary Survey 2015: A Younger Workforce, Still Predominantly White," *PublishersWeekly.com*, October 16, 2015, http://www.publishersweekly.com/pw/by-topic/industry-news/publisher-news/article/68405-publishing-industry-salary-survey-2015-a-younger-workforce-still-predominantly-white.html.

9   Haeyoun Park Keller Josh and Josh Williams, "The Faces of American Power, Nearly as White as the Oscar Nominees," *The New York Times*, February 26, 2016, http://www.nytimes.com/interactive/2016/02/26/us/race-of-american-power.html.

than just basic mechanics; instead they want them to ask meaningful questions and challenge the information they find. But it can be hard for librarians who've just discovered critical information literacy to figure out how to teach it. Even experienced critical librarians often run into roadblocks to teaching with critical methods. Sometimes they feel uncomfortable bringing in critical methods when working with particular professors or they may decide there is not enough time due to the large amount of content they need to introduce.

Finding ways to include critical content in classes is often simpler and can require far less time in the class session. It can be an easier entry point for librarians trying to be critical teachers than jumping straight into the deep end of critical pedagogy. Librarians who do teach with critical methods usually teach at least some critical content in those sessions. Critical information literacy classes are usually focused on helping students understand the research process and information cycles and flows. Critical librarians understand that students enter the class with well-formed opinions about the media, the Internet, and information, and many have preconceived notions about the library, librarians, and the research process. Librarians should embrace this by using that background to help students expand on what they already know and challenge them to consider new ideas in relation to old ones. This chapter will present the types of critical content my study participants included in their sessions.

Critical evaluation was front and center in many critical information literacy sessions. Several participants urged students to pose questions of the sources they found to help them discover that the production of all kinds of information is done within a sociopolitical system, and the creation and dissemination of information has to be considered within that system. Franks advised librarians to,

> challenge students to ask themselves: as information is situated through the publication hierarchy, discussed initially, perhaps on the web, placed within academic journals, and then introductory works like encyclopedias, how are decisions made about what should be represented and as information is carefully filtered out for the more selective publications and sliced up for recombination and redefinition, what is deemed important enough to include and why? Who is supported by such decisions in terms of

both disciplinary boundaries and the larger hierarchy of social power?[10]

Most participants had goals around doing what Franks suggested. Some were able to do this sometimes, but a smaller number found ways to make this type of content prominent in the majority of their instruction sessions. Librarians who made critical content prominent had often grounded their instruction sessions in the theories of critical information studies, cultural studies, or critical literacy before discovering critical information literacy. These theories seem promising for helping other librarians find concrete ways to incorporate critical content into their teaching. They also look at how the social, political, and economic nature and presentation of information creates and/or reinforces cultures.[11] Further, critical literacy and cultural studies scholars have been refining their praxis for decades longer than critical information literacy scholars, which provides librarians with a rich set of scholarship to draw from.

CRITICAL SOURCE EVALUATION: THE EXCLUSION OF VOICES

The types of critical content that librarians most often teach are concepts related to and involving source evaluation, subject headings, and other issues of language in finding and using information. Critical source evaluation can be taught as just one part of an information literacy session or it can be the core concept of a session, with everything else, including methods and other content, based around or in relation to source evaluation. After trying different methods and content in his semester-long information literacy course for a few semesters, Matthew decided to turn his entire course into "an

10   S. Franks, "Grand Narratives and the Information Cycle in the Library Instruction Classroom," in *Critical Library Instruction: Theories and Methods*, ed. Maria T. Accardi, Emily Drabinski, and Alana Kumbier (Duluth, MN: Library Juice Press, 2010), 46.

11   H. Inokuchi and Y. Nozaki, "Critical Approach to Asia through Library Collections and Instruction in North America: Selection of Culture and Counter-Hegemonic Library Practices," in *Critical Library Instruction: Theories and Methods*, ed. Maria T. Accardi, Emily Drabinski, and Alana Kumbier (Duluth, MN: Library Juice Press, 2010), 237-48; Siva Vaidhyanathan, "Afterword: Critical Information Studies," *Cultural Studies* 20, no. 2/3 (May 3, 2006): 292-315, doi:10.1080/09502380500521091.

evaluation course." At the other end of the spectrum, librarians teach critical source evaluation as part of one-shot sessions in freshman year programs or for classes within the disciplines. Critical source evaluation is usually taught from one of two angles: librarians either teach topics related to how knowledge is produced and disseminated or they problematize the hard distinction librarians and scholars often make between scholarly and popular sources. While it may be possible to teach both of these ideas in one class, it would be hard to go in-depth on both in a single session.

K NOWLEDGE   P RODUCTION   AND   D ISSEMINATION

Teaching about the production and dissemination of knowledge includes looking at elements such as politics, economics, class, power, and other sociocultural aspects of information. Framing descriptions of critical source evaluation within the context of social justice, including the power and economic structures implicit in information creation and dissemination, can be very powerful for students. When teaching about the power relations involved in information structures, librarians can use language that will hook the students into the conversation and ignite a personal response. Pointing out that "people are trying to manipulate you," "information is for sale," and "information is a commodity" were common tactics of my participants, as was asking students to consider "who [owns] the voices that we are listening to," and to think about the immense "power in research."[12] Encouraging students to be cognizant of the voices that are privileged and not privileged in both academic research and in other types of information and media is a principle concern of critical information literacy.

Students are often woefully limited in their understanding about the political nature of information. Teachers and librarians make the problem worse when they present simplified evaluation checklists, which often imply that subscription databases are neutral or the best place to access unbiased information. I have begun many discussions with students about the importance of evaluation only to be cut off with desperately bored looks and the occasional comment about learning about this since middle school. Students think they

---

12   These are all phrases that study participants used to describe power relations implicit in information production and dissemination processes in order to hook students into the conversation.

already know all they need to know about evaluation by the time they make it to college. And they *have* learned about it in high school, but what they have learned is often the most rudimentary start of the evaluation conversation. So our job in the college library classroom becomes two-fold: first, we have to convince them that they've only learned the first part; and second, we have to present the complicated nuances of comprehensive critical evaluation.

In his instruction sessions in support of research paper assignments, Daniel, a community college librarian, hoped to get students to think about the voices in different sources and to evaluate information based at least partly on those voices. To do that, he focused on the process of creating and disseminating information and research, encouraging students to view it as a conversation. Like many librarians teaching critical evaluation, Daniel struggled with the challenge of how to actually accomplish such a large goal within the context of a simple, lower level undergraduate research paper assignment and the constraints of a one-shot instruction session. But he reasoned that librarians cannot really expect students to make all of the connections we want them to make in our short sessions anyway. In terms of rich and deep content, the most we can hope is to plant seeds so that students will begin to think about the ideas. We will likely not be there when something we've presented or talked about in a library session comes alive for them. As Daniel stated,

> I'm trying to emphasize to students these kinds of core concepts of where information comes from; who the voices are that we are listening to; that all sources are the voice of somebody; and all conversations have people that are included and people that are excluded. And are we recognizing how that conversation is going on?
>
> Sometimes those are big things to get into a student's head when you're talking about an eight or five page paper with three or four sources. How much conversation are they really going to get access to when they are only reading three or four sources...Hopefully there's larger projects in the future when students transfer or they're in their subject matter coursework that are going to open them up to different kinds of stuff.

William taught about the political aspects of information by trying to "find a way to get [students] to think about what's not in the database." Looking at concepts, ideas, and voices that are excluded is an excellent way to help students understand that information and knowledge are not neutral things. Rather, they are disseminated as part of an agenda and within a larger context. As an education librarian, William thought it was important to help students understand that even the most comprehensive and respected education database is not necessarily neutral because it is supported by the national government and focuses on mainstream content.

> Within education, I talk about ERIC and how the database was scrubbed during the Bush Administration to exclude a lot of critical and qualitative education studies and journals. And how some of the best critical education periodicals like Rethinking Schools aren't indexed anywhere other than the Alternative Press Index, which doesn't make it onto most university library databases because of money...I get them to think about how politics and economics affect the information that's presented and how it's presented and at least to get them to begin to question this and not think that just whatever is there is what there is.

Some librarians find it helpful to draw on the scholarship of critical information studies to develop class discussions around issues of power and social justice in the creation, production, and consumption of information. Critical information studies is cross-disciplinary and offers concrete structures as points for analysis that are relevant to all disciplines of study. According to Vaidhyanatha, critical information studies "interrogates the structures, functions, habits, norms, and practices that guide global flows of information...[and] asks questions about access, costs, and chilling effects on, within, and among audiences, citizens, emerging cultural creators, indigenous cultural groups, teachers, and students."[13] This includes looking at things like copyright, digital access issues, and the importance of sharing scholarship across disciplinary lines and taking down the walls that separate academic scholarship and the public.

Shari, a foreign languages librarian at a large state university, worked to help students understand the global nature of information.

---

13   Vaidhyanathan, "Afterword," 1.

She wanted them to learn how to identify and respond to power relations affecting the production and accessibility of information relevant to the people they were studying. She used critical information studies to shape the content of many of her classes, especially as she learned about and delved more deeply into critical information literacy. Shari was "trying to teach students ... to think about...voices [and] social justice...and to question who is contributing to Wikipedia [and other sources. For example], why is it that there's people in Argentina who are writing about Bolivia?"

Other participants also used Wikipedia in their discussions on critical source evaluation for several reasons. First and foremost, students use it extensively so it is a source that they are all familiar with, therefore it provides a common experience to ground a class discussion. In a 2009 study,[14] 85% of students admitted to using Wikipedia when starting their research to help them formulate a basic understanding and create context for their topic. Secondly, it is an important source for students to understand because they are using it in a foundational way. That is, they are essentially using it to provide the basic framework for their research. Finally, it is a source that is full of political implications: it is available for free on the Internet, it is created and edited by credentialed and non-credentialed people with different goals,[15] it is frequently manipulated with negative aims,[16] and is guided by a robust set of policy guidelines that impact its quality and credibility.[17]

Participants addressed several of these issues when they discussed it in classes. For example, Matthew talked to students about the purpose of Wikipedia, including who drives that purpose. Wikipedia presents itself as a source written by and for the people, but it has a lot

---

14   Alison J. Head and Michael B. Eisenberg, "What Today's College Students Say about Conducting Research in the Digital Age," 2009, http://www.libraryng.com/sites/libraryng.com/files/PIL_ProgressReport_2_2009.pdf.

15   Nicholas Carr, "Deletionists, Inclusionists and Delusionists," *ROUGH TYPE*, September 5, 2006, http://www.roughtype.com/?p=525.

16   Associated Press, "Political Dirty-Tricksters Using Wikipedia," *MSNBC.com*, April 28, 2006, http://www.nbcnews.com/id/12535412/ns/politics/t/political-dirty-tricksters-using-wikipedia/.

17   Olof Sundin, "Janitors of Knowledge: Constructing Knowledge in the Everyday Life of Wikipedia Editors," *Journal of Documentation* 67, no. 5 (2011): 840-62, doi:10.1108/00220411111164709.

of rules around credibility and quality, such as citing scholarly sources in its entries and sometimes even requiring senior editors to approve edits before they go live.[18] In addition to other discussions they may have had around Wikipedia, all of the participants who included it in their classes used it to explore and challenge the dichotomies of bad versus good and scholarly versus popular sources.

Scholarly v. Popular (Good v. Bad)

The scholarly versus popular dichotomy is a common concept in librarianship. Librarians have discussed it for several years in journal articles, at conferences, and on blogs and listservs, mostly focusing on how this concept can be effectively explained to students. In order to convey the difference between scholarly and popular resources, librarians explain it in classes and create research guides and checklists for students to use to help them make the distinction. The problem is that students have interpreted this message of privileging scholarly sources over popular ones as librarians and professors telling them that scholarly equals good and popular equals bad.[19]

Recent discussions have started to shift, as librarians have finally started to question the assumption that scholarly sources are automatically better, realizing that they have presented problematic black or white thinking to students rather than encouraging them to critically evaluate all of their sources.[20] Because of her discovery of critical information literacy, Lily changed her practice from the checklist method of presenting information as good versus bad and stopped encouraging students to automatically and mindlessly privilege elite academic voices.

Peer review was another problematic concept for some participants because they felt that it—along with the designation "scholarly journal"—often leads students to think that if they check

---

18   Dariusz Jemielniak, *Common Knowledge? : An Ethnography of Wikipedia* (Stanford, CA: Stanford University Press, 2014).

19   Amy E. Mark, "Format as a False Judge of Credibility: Messages from Librarians and Faculty and Student Responses," Communications in Information Literacy 5, no. 1 (2011): 21-37, http://www.comminfolit.org/index.php?journal=cil&page=article&op=viewFile&path%5B%5D=v5i1p21&path%5B%5D=127.

20   Candice B. Small, "Re: Explaining Scholarly Resources," *ILI-L Discussion List*, November 9, 2013, http://lists.ala.org/sympa/arc/ili-l/2013-11/msg00067.html.

the peer-reviewed box in a database, their evaluative work is done. Students are taught that this means they now have a "good" source that their professor will approve of and it never occurs to them that they may need to do some more digging[21] to find out if there is bias in the article, if the author or the journal has an agenda of some kind, who funded the study, and all of the other questions that students should be asking about each source they find.

In order to get students to think about sources in ways other than just good or bad, or scholarly or popular, some participants taught them to choose sources based on the purpose of what they were trying to do or encouraged them to develop questions and helped them think through how to find more information in the pursuit of answers. For example, Kate tried to stress developing questions with students rather than focusing only on article evaluation. She believed it was more meaningful for students to think about the big picture of scholarship creation and how that process works than to focus on single bits of information and trying to determine reliability and credibility in isolation. She tried different methods to accomplish this, including developing a process of viewing and evaluating the web as "a series of primary texts," because she argued that "in the humanities, these are the primary texts that we are reading today."

Matthew also focused on process and had become reluctant to push students to use specific tools without helping them to think deeply about the types of questions they wished to answer and the purposes of types of sources rather than privileging certain formats and tools over others. He wanted to help students think more critically about the whole process, so instead of saying, "'you have a research project? Here's the catalog; [I'll] help you use it.'...[He would say] 'you have a research project? Can the catalog help you in this particular circumstance?'" He argued that librarians and professors should encourage students to think beyond form:

> We should be looking at things in terms of what it is that they are trying to do. So looking at scholarship: it tries to do this and it takes various forms. It can be in the form of a journal article; it can take the form of a book; newspapers

21   Mark, "Format as a False Judge of Credibility: Messages from Librarians and Faculty and Student Responses."

attempt to do this and it can be in the form of a website [or] a newspaper [or] a web app. It doesn't matter what form it's in, it matters what it's attempting to do. And helping students differentiate those purposes... because if they can understand...the choices that are out there then they can adopt those choices for themselves.

SUBJECT HEADINGS AND LANGUAGE

The second major category of critical content typical in critical information literacy sessions are topics related to the language used in searching mechanisms, such as the subject headings and keywords in library catalogs and databases and the importance of language and terminology in searching the Internet. Biased, racist, sexist, and generally outdated classifications have been a known problem in librarianship since at least the late 1960s when Sanford Berman argued in a letter to the editor of *Library Journal* "that the Library of Congress Subject Headings represent a white racist imperialist point of view." [22]

The main type of critical content that Jane included in her information literacy classes was problematizing subject headings in the library catalog. She used examples or created conversations with students that illustrated the questionable classification or outright exclusion of different populations in the catalog. She found that focusing on subject headings was a good entry point for helping students see the political nature of information organization.

> I teach a lot with subject headings. We'll look at the record and then talk about the subject headings. [I ask students:] What is contained in those headings? And what isn't? What are some other words you can use? [For example, in a] public health...class, the students were researching different populations and some of them could find stuff and some of them couldn't. We talked about why they couldn't [and] why populations aren't studied and named.

---

22   A.C. Foskett, "Misogynists All: A Study in Critical Classification," *Library Resources and Technical Services* 15, no. 2 (1971): 121.

Linda was similarly interested in problematizing subject headings with students by looking at how different groups were classified and defined. She advocated inserting little bits of critical content, such as leading a quick discussion of whether there is a distinct subject heading for men authors like there is for women authors or something else relevant to the course that shows some of the sociopolitical nature of information organization.

Matthew also worked with students to discover the underlying language of information sources and structures. He focused less on the library catalog and more on how keywords were constructed and functioned in subject-specific library databases and on the Internet. He framed these discussions in terms of how disciplinary languages work and how language reflects and is a function of the purpose of the source. He wanted students to understand that "the way that someone describes [something] matters...[I]f you google 'estate tax,' you get stuff from the IRS,...*Forbes,* [and the] *Wall Street Journal.* If you google 'death tax,' which is the same thing, you get NoTaxes.org, LifeAndLiberty.org...[and a] series of conservative-oriented websites that are basically 'abolish the death tax.'"

Matthew used a similar strategy to analyze Wikipedia. One method he used was to write slang terms for marijuana on the board and ask students, "who uses these terms?" Of course, the students would say "potheads" or "stoners." So then he asked what words scientists used and the students answered with things like "marijuana, cannabis, cannabinoid, THC." Then he showed them that Wikipedia uses cannabis and asked them why. The students reasoned it was because Wikipedia wants to be taken seriously, which he then countered with "[I]f Wikipedia is the will of the people so to speak, then why are they using these more clinical terms? [Does it] illustrate that they want people coming to Wikipedia to take it seriously?"

Conclusion

In his fascinating ethnography of Wikipedia, Jemielniak observed that "many academics object to Wikipedia merely because it challenges the traditional social construction of knowledge and its dissemination, in which the empowered academics are the ones who play the roles of crucial gatekeepers and disseminators."[23] The tension around Wikipedia between students and faculty provides an interesting illustration of the power imbalance between students and faculty and how their ongoing power struggle has been magnified by the availability of online information. Most college students are prepared to tell you about the problems with Wikipedia—that it can be changed, regular people write the articles (not experts), and it is not properly vetted for accuracy—but they don't believe those arguments. They use it, like it, and trust it.

The same goes for Google. Students don't believe librarians and faculty when we tell them that they will find more resources in the library's subscription databases because their experience has not backed up that assertion. So once again, our challenge as librarians is to teach them to think about both the tools they use to find content and the content itself—not to simply convince them to use what we've bought. There are those that argue that " the new mode of knowledge production surpasses the traditional, hierarchical, turf-driven, and caste like system that universities depend on."[24] There is some truth to this assertion, but it is also true that new hierarchies and fiefdoms tend to pop up anywhere that humans are involved. Our job as librarians is to teach students that that is the case for information, as it is for other human endeavors. Information is not neutral because it is created through social means. Deeply investigating sources and content allows students to see and involve themselves in the social and political aspects of information creation, enabling them to make better decisions about everything, including whether to be afraid of Ebola or to start a social media campaign demanding equal representation at the Oscars.

---

23 Dariusz Jemielniak, *Common Knowledge?*, 184.

24 Ibid., 185.

Works Cited

Associated Press. "Political Dirty-Tricksters Using Wikipedia." *MSNBC.com*, April 28, 2006. http://www.nbcnews.com/id/12535412/ns/politics/t/political-dirty-tricksters-using-wikipedia/.

Carr, Nicholas. "Deletionists, Inclusionists and Delusionists." *ROUGH TYPE*, September 5, 2006. http://www.roughtype.com/?p=525.

Day, Elizabeth. "#BlackLivesMatter: The Birth of a New Civil Rights Movement." *The Guardian*, July 19, 2015, sec. World news. http://www.theguardian.com/world/2015/jul/19/blacklives-matter-birth-civil-rights-movement.

Foskett, A.C. "Misogynists All: A Study in Critical Classification." *Library Resources and Technical Services* 15, no. 2 (1971): 117-21.

Franks, S. "Grand Narratives and the Information Cycle in the Library Instruction Classroom." In *Critical Library Instruction: Theories and Methods*, edited by Maria T. Accardi, Emily Drabinski, and Alana Kumbier, 43-54. Duluth, MN: Library Juice Press, 2010.

Head, Alison J., and Michael B. Eisenberg. "What Today's College Students Say about Conducting Research in the Digital Age," 2009. http://www.libraryng.com/sites/libraryng.com/files/PIL_ProgressReport_2_2009.pdf.

Inokuchi, H., and Y. Nozaki. "Critical Approach to Asia through Library Collections and Instruction in North America: Selection of Culture and Counter-Hegemonic Library Practices." In *Critical Library Instruction: Theories and Methods*, edited by Maria T. Accardi, Emily Drabinski, and Alana Kumbier, 237-48. Duluth, MN: Library Juice Press, 2010.

Jemielniak, Dariusz . *Common Knowledge?: An Ethnography of Wikipedia*. Stanford, CA: Stanford University Press, 2014.

Maharidge, Dale. "These Journalists Dedicated Their Lives to Telling Other People's Stories. What Happens When No One Wants to Print Their Words Anymore?" *The Nation*, March 2, 2016. http://www.thenation.com/article/these-journalists-dedicated-their-lives-to-telling-other-peoples-stories/.

Mark, Amy E. "Format as a False Judge of Credibility: Messages from Librarians and Faculty and Student Responses." Communications in Information Literacy 5, no. 1 (2011): 21–37. http://www.comminfolit.org/index.php?journal=cil&page=article&op=viewFile&path%5B%5D=v5i1p21&path%5B%5D=127.

Milliot, Jim. "The PW Publishing Industry Salary Survey 2015: A Younger Workforce, Still Predominantly White." *PublishersWeekly.com*, October 16, 2015. http://www.publishersweekly.com/pw/by-topic/industry-news/publisher-news/article/68405-publishing-industry-salary-survey-2015-a-younger-workforce-still-predominantly-white.html.

Park, Haeyoun, Josh Keller, and Josh Williams. "The Faces of American Power, Nearly as White as the Oscar Nominees." *The New York Times*, February 26, 2016. http://www.nytimes.com/interactive/2016/02/26/us/race-of-american-power.html.

Saad, Lydia. "Ebola Ranks Among Americans' Top Three Healthcare Concerns." *Gallup.com*. Accessed March 4, 2016. http://www.gallup.com/poll/179429/ebola-ranks-among-americans-top-three-healthcare-concerns.aspx.

Small, Candice B. "Re: Explaining Scholarly Resources." *ILI-L Discussion List*, November 9, 2013. http://lists.ala.org/sympa/arc/ili-l/2013-11/msg00067.html.

Small, Len. "Nothing Snowballs Online Like Fear." *Nautilus*, February 18, 2016. http://nautil.us/issue/33/attraction/how-ebola-infected-twitter.

Sundin, Olof. "Janitors of Knowledge: Constructing Knowledge in the Everyday Life of Wikipedia Editors." *Journal of Documentation* 67, no. 5 (2011): 840-62. doi:10.1108/00220411111164709.

Vaidhyanathan, Siva. "Afterword: Critical Information Studies." *Cultural Studies* 20, no. 2/3 (May 3, 2006): 292-315. doi:10.1080/09502380500521091.

CHAPTER 6

CREATING A SUPPORTIVE TEACHING CULTURE FOR
LIBRARIANS: INSTITUTIONALIZING (CRITICAL)
INFORMATION LITERACY

In recent decades, many colleges and universities have put substantial resources into creating a "culture of teaching" on their campuses.[1] The evidence that institutional support from administrators and relationships with colleagues heavily impacts how teachers teach[2] has prompted administrators to encourage a campus wide commitment to teaching excellence and meaningful assessment.[3] Unfortunately, even though librarians are also better teachers when they have institutional support,[4] they have generally been left out of most institution-wide instructional improvement programs and do not enjoy much institutional support for their teaching duties.[5]

---

1 Bradley E. Cox et al., "A Culture of Teaching: Policy, Perception, and Practice in Higher Education," *Research in Higher Education* 52, no. 8 (December 2011): 808–29, doi:10.1007/s11162-011-9223-6.

2 Alan Jenkins and Michael Healey, *Institutional Strategies to Link Teaching and Research* (York: Higher Education Academy, 2005), http://www.vision2020.gu.se/digitalAssets/1345/1345048_institutional_strategies.pdf.

3 Cox et al., "A Culture of Teaching."

4 Sharon A. Weiner, "Institutionalizing Information Literacy," *The Journal of Academic Librarianship* 38, no. 5 (September 2012): 287–93, doi:10.1016/j.acalib.2012.05.004.

5 Walter Scott, "Instructional Improvement: Building Capacity for the Professional Development of Librarians as Teachers," *Reference & User Services Quarterly* 45, no. 3 (Spring 2006): 213–18.

Even with institutional support, critical information literacy is difficult to implement. Collaborative relationships with faculty and colleagues can help librarians put it into practice. Additionally, the project of critical information literacy is important for all students and in most, if not all, disciplines, so the work to expand it should fall to the wider educational community—not librarians alone. The level of expansion needed is only possible with support and advocacy from administrators. In this chapter, I will discuss some obstacles to critical information literacy, provide a picture of the support librarians receive from faculty, colleagues, and administrators at their institutions, and present ideas for overcoming obstacles and expanding support.

Too Little Time, Not Enough Vision: Overcoming Obstacles to Institutional Expansion

Expanding critical information literacy at the institutional level will heavily depend on administrative support, faculty relationships, and changing internal and external perceptions of academic librarianship. However, critical librarians face some sizable obstacles to expansion. I am following Henry's lead by breaking these into two types: practical issues, such as limited staffing, financial and other resources, and time; and turf issues that arise when working with faculty, and librarians' roles and vision for themselves in the education process.

Practical Issues

Practical issues are those things on campus that make doing anything new or different challenging, including staffing, resources, time, and organizational matters. Just as inadequate staffing impedes innovation in other parts of the library, it does the same for teaching. Shari felt lack of staff was one of the big obstacles to the growth of information literacy at her institution. Critical information literacy takes time and as a liaison to several departments at a large university, time limitations sometimes kept Shari from trying out new things. Andrea was facing similar issues related to understaffing. Her library had not replaced librarians and other library staff as they retired or left the institution, which led to those left getting "a lot more focused on what we need to do...[and] so busy in doing our own little jobs, we don't have enough time to think about the overarching thing."

Lack of time was a major issue for most of my study participants. Several said the lack of time made it difficult to develop new teaching methods and plans. Those teaching primarily first year programs were more likely to state that their overwhelming instructional load made it hard for them to try new approaches in the classroom or even to have time to reflect very much on what they were already doing. Jane said of the first year instructional program she organized, that "it's such a high volume operation that we very rarely step back to talk, to reflect."

Another practical issue is the context of the university itself. A small number of participants thought this context did not lend itself to being able to enact true critical pedagogy of any kind, including critical information literacy. Eva thought that there are too many institutional limitations in the modern corporate university model to make critical pedagogy possible. She argued that the purpose, content, and structure of the classroom is decided well before she sees a class, which presents constraints that cannot be overcome:

> There's a lot of lip service paid to critical pedagogy in the university. And even people who I greatly admire—I admire their politics, I admire their research, I admire them as teachers to a point—their classroom looks just like any other classroom and I'm not going to change that going in three times. That's not possible. That can't happen.

TURF ISSUES

Another common set of obstacles that librarians must deal with involve turf issues, which largely revolve around working with faculty and relate to librarians' reluctance to be seen as intruding on faculty territory, while still managing to do important and meaningful pedagogical work. Henry felt that librarians tend to struggle with finding a balance between being a relevant educational partner with professors and not overstepping the boundaries of what they believe to be their role because they "don't want to be seen as encroaching on...the prerogative and expertise of the disciplinary faculty. We want to be seen as knowledgeable and helpful partners and there's no real cookbook method for that...you just have to build these relationships and build trust."

Matthew argued that librarians often "don't have the opportunity to stretch our wings and do things that might not be expected of us." He was concerned that information literacy is often "not seen as anything that important," because it is not a standalone discipline, which further contributes to the difficulties librarians may face if they try to expand their role or push their teaching in different directions. He thought information literacy is seen as "sort of this extra thing on top of" the important subjects, which puts us in "this weird position where what we do is absolutely important and necessary for students to learn and understand for success. [But] we don't have a venue or a platform to actually drive that point home."

Librarians must grow beyond traditional roles if we hope to expand critical information literacy. Lily argued for expanding roles, but she thought being able to do so was the biggest obstacle librarians face because "the job of librarians is to help and support faculty and students in their research and learning [and]...for a long time that meant providing a service." But she believed librarians' roles are and should be changing:

> I feel like the obstacles...are really in the educational role that we take on. ...[Some] librarians are fulfilling their educational role [with] the status quo, and teaching the library as databases and helping students make sense of the physical space of the library by providing tours. To me that's the lowest threshold of our instructional capacity. And because our educational role ...[relies] on our ability to partner with people who are carrying out the act of teaching within the curriculum, going beyond that role is, in some cases, challenging to our partners. And so I think we constantly have to have that awareness of how can we do our work to contribute to student learning while also pushing these boundaries. And when you bring critical information literacy into play, you're talking about pushing boundaries in ways that could be perceived as inappropriate. It can be perceived as beyond the scope of what we should be doing.

The roles librarians have traditionally occupied limits not only what others expect from us, but also what we expect from ourselves. Several participants felt a substantial contributor to librarians' difficulties in expanding their roles came from the way librarians view themselves.

Eva said that librarians at her institution often say they don't feel respected even though many of the librarians she works with have second masters' degrees and PhDs. She thought a lot of this came from the librarians, not from faculty and administrators. She argued that "there's this kind of experience of being lesser than that librarians often have." Anna talked about an experience she had at an ACRL Information Literacy Immersion Program, which is an intensive multi-day workshop for academic librarians to develop and build teaching skills. She was surprised to hear from so many librarians attending the program that they did not identify as teachers.

> I went to intentional teaching immersion last year, and one thing that I thought was interesting was that a lot of my colleagues there said that they really didn't identify themselves as teachers for the most part... Half said, "Yes, I am a teacher" and half said "I'm a trainer" or "I show people how to do things" and didn't necessarily have that type of teaching identity. I think that that might be an issue...that might keep some people away from critical information literacy, is just not feeling like you have the agency or the authority to be engaged in this kind of stuff if you don't even really feel like you are a teacher.

I will look more closely at the culture of librarianship as a profession in the next chapter, including how we often get in our own way when it comes to our work with faculty and administrators.

THE MOST DECISIVE FACTOR? FACULTY RELATIONSHIPS

In 1958, Knapp argued that,

> Neither subject field, nor teaching method, nor kind of assignment, nor quality of student in a class is of crucial importance in determining whether or not a given course will be dependent on the library. The only decisive factor seemed to be—and this is a subjective judgment—the instructor's

attitude. Where the instructor expected and planned for student use, it occurred. Where he did not, it did not occur.[6]

Over fifty years later, the experiences of the librarians in my study mirrored Knapp's take on the importance of the teaching faculty member in determining the role the library plays in terms of student use for a course. Numerous studies have shown that the majority of professors think *libraries* are important in the education of students, but they do not value the role of *librarians* in the educational process. In keeping with this view, the overwhelming majority of faculty members do not invite librarians into their classes to provide instruction.[7] Therefore, it is not surprising that building relationships with the teaching faculty is of the utmost importance to librarians and they are very careful with the relationships they develop.

All of the librarians I interviewed spoke to some degree about the importance of librarian and faculty relationships. As Lily said, "our educational role hinges...on our ability to partner with people who are carrying out the act of teaching within the curriculum." They all also described at least some positive relationships with faculty members, but most still tended to tread lightly when it came to introducing new ideas or using methods or content that may be perceived as pushing the boundaries of their traditional roles.

Members of the teaching faculty often have a limited understanding of librarians' roles and responsibilities. Walter found in his study of faculty perceptions of librarian work that "relatively few faculty members were aware of the range of instructional responsibilities held by many academic librarians, and many did not consider teaching to be a significant responsibility for librarians when compared with other responsibilities that they associated with the profession."[8] Most of my participants did not try to introduce critical concepts or methods unless they had worked with the professor before and felt like they had a good relationship already in place. They tried

---

6   As cited by Kate Manuel, Susan E. Beck, and Molly Molloy, "An Ethnographic Study of Attitudes Influencing Faculty Collaboration in Library Instruction," *Reference Librarian* 43, no. 89-90 (April 27, 2005): 140, doi:10.1300/J120v43n89_10.

7   Manuel, Beck, and Molloy, "An Ethnographic Study of Attitudes Influencing Faculty Collaboration in Library Instruction."

8   Scott Walter, "Librarians as Teachers: A Qualitative Inquiry into Professional Identity," *College & Research Libraries* 69, no. 1 (2008): 60, http://crl.acrl.org.

to cultivate relationships over the long term, building patience and trust among faculty members. Linda observed that, "it's a long process to build relationships where the faculty members have some trust in the librarian and respect the librarian's knowledge, and the librarian has to do it in a graceful way."

Andrea also took a long view, saying that what she was "doing has sort of evolved over the years." Like several of the librarians, she often worked with people for many years and made gradual changes each semester, building on what she had done in the past. She also believed she may have a special advantage because "sometimes people in my department trust me, because...I taught in the English department that I do library sessions for. So they know me and they know that I know their curriculum." She thought they often gave her more "free reign" because of that, which contrasted with her experience with her other liaison area, the history department. It took more time for her to gain the trust of that department's faculty so that she could exercise more freedom in the classroom.

Department level initiatives and relationships are especially important and are key to expanding critical information literacy. Information literacy is more integrated in some academic departments than others, both in and across institutions. Information literacy instruction is much more effective in departments that value it because the faculty in those departments reinforce its importance with students, collaborate more with librarians on developing good curriculum, provide more feedback on improvements, and provide time and space in their course to focus on information literacy.

Disciplinary Considerations

Grounding information literacy within a disciplinary context is an important aspect of developing critical information literacy. "An understanding of signature disciplinary pedagogies, where they exist, helps librarians to embed either themselves or valuable content into teaching and learning experiences."[9] As Jaguszewski and Williams point out in their 2013 Association of Research Libraries report on the changing roles of liaisons, librarians have to tie their instruction in

---

9   Janice Jaguszewski and Karen Williams, "New Roles for New Times: Transforming Liaison Roles in Research Libraries," 2013, http://conservancy.umn.edu/handle/11299/169867.

with the structure of the disciplines they support to be effective. Some disciplines use case studies, others teach primarily in a lab, others rely on traditional modes of teaching and research, and so forth. The majority of those I interviewed agreed that information literacy should be taught within the disciplines.

Michael asserted that "integrating information literacy into the disciplines would be the better approach" than continuing to follow the old model of teaching decontextualized information literacy skills based on general standards, such as the *ACRL Standards*. Matthew argued that keeping information literacy separate from the disciplines pointed to librarians "having a stunted understanding of what research is." He believed that while they know and can articulate its importance, librarians often misinterpret the significance of teaching with context to mean only the context of an assignment, rather than the broader context of disciplinary and scholarly communication. The context of the discipline influenced the critical information literacy practice of participants in two ways: first, the nature of the discipline contributed to how they taught and how effective they thought the instruction was; and second, it provided a disciplinary discourse through which they could introduce critical information literacy content.

NATURE OF THE DISCIPLINE

Several participants thought critical information literacy worked better in some disciplines than others. However, there was not always agreement on which disciplines presented challenges. For example, Lily thought that critical information literacy did not work as well in the sciences, while Matthew experienced a lot of success when introducing critical source evaluation in the sciences. The disciplines that participants stated it worked well for included Latin American studies, nursing, biology, business, English, communication studies, anthropology, history, psychology, women and gender studies, chemistry, education, and humanities.

Andrea taught critical content to a large number of history classes, which she believed was a good fit because "history students really do an awful lot of research in the library and in the archives." Lily had success with communication studies and gender and women's studies because they were open to having critical conversations about the nature and structure of information sources. Linda believed she was successful at bringing critical content into some of the humanities classes she had worked with because those disciplines "tend to have a more critical theory approach in terms of their discipline, so there was an openness to bringing in more theoretical sorts of ideas into the classes."

The disciplines that individual librarians struggled with introducing critical information literacy concepts to included the professional disciplines, English, humanities, sciences, and divinity. Anna thought it was more difficult to teach it to humanities students because "there is not much of a concrete problem that [she could] ask them to solve." William believed that some disciplines have a more obvious tie-in to critical information literacy than others, providing "clear examples and examples that are relevant and hit home," as opposed to disciplines that are less political in nature and are less interested in the economics of information. For example, he thought the divinity students he worked with were not interested in examining information in that way because "there's a couple of key databases that they go to and...politics and economics doesn't enter into it quite as much...it's more theology and theological viewpoints." Whereas, he saw more of an entry point for these types of discussions in psychology and he "had the most success with education."

It makes sense that differences among disciplines may impact librarians' ability to introduce critical information literacy concepts and methods. "[D]isciplinary differences have a significant influence on the ways in which academic work is organized,"[10] creating different goals, teaching methods, ways of interacting with students, approaches to research, and so forth. All of these elements contribute to creating wholly different academic environments that encompass more than just the different subject matter taught by each.[11] Chris explained how these differences may show up for professional disciplines:

> [T]he more professional disciplines are going to be motivated on...an instrumental sort of knowledge. First, you've really got to know your stuff. There's key empirical questions or

---

10 Paul Gorsky, et al., "The Relationship between Academic Discipline and Dialogic Behavior in Open University Course Forums," *International Review of Research in Open and Distance Learning* 11, no. 2 (May 5, 2010): 51, http://www.irrodl.org/index.php.

11 Armin Krishnan, "What Are Academic Disciplines? Some Observations on the Disciplinarity vs. Interdisciplinarity Debate," NCRM Working Paper Series (University of Southampton National Centre for Research Methods, 2009), http://www.forschungsnetzwerk.at/downloadpub/what_are_academic_disciplines2009.pdf.

key empirical information that you just have to know in order to provide those professional services...I try to do a lot of outreach to the economics department, for example, and I've found some economists who will assign research papers, but others [are] doing exam models. There's heavy quantitative sorts of things to what they're teaching.

Disciplinary Discourse

Several participants thought their success with critical information literacy was largely because it fit with the discourse of the discipline they were working with. "Disciplinary discourse includes the ways that members of a particular discourse community write, read, speak, and research, as well as the assumptions that they make and the epistemologies with which they craft their arguments."[12] Jane was a proponent of teaching within the disciplines because she thought it provided the context to have critical conversations as part of the discipline's discourse and had more meaning to students:

> I don't know how you teach about information without a context that [students] care about. And I know many people in their majors don't care about their majors but... a) I think you're more likely to get students who do care and b) I think the context is there to talk about information literacy. So I have a much easier time using a critical language and developing a critical classroom practice in a major course than I do in freshman comp because I think the context is there for talking about disciplinary knowledge creation.

Shari thought that her work with the Spanish department provided a lot of opportunities for her to introduce critical information concepts because the students in those courses were reading texts and information that was not about the dominant culture in which they lived. Therefore, to develop a better understanding of those cultures, their discipline required them to investigate the social and cultural construction of information, including analyzing who

---

12 Michelle Holschuh Simmons, "Librarians as Disciplinary Discourse Mediators: Using Genre Theory to Move toward Critical Information Literacy," *portal: Libraries & the Academy* 5, no. 3 (2005): 297.

the dominant voices were that provided their understanding of the cultures they were engaged with.

Some participants learned about critical theories or critical pedagogy because it was part of the disciplinary discourses of the academic disciplines that they were liaisons to. For example, Kate began talking about many of the theories that fit under the critical umbrella before realizing there was such a thing as critical information literacy because "a lot of the theories are just part of the practice of the discipline and so some of these ideas ended up getting in the information literacy class because...they became part of what I did." Lily had a similar experience; she worked with students who were studying feminist and other critical theories in the classes she interacted with in her role as liaison to gender and women's studies. She actually first learned about critical theory from a professor that she taught for in the same program so her insertion of critical information literacy into her instruction sessions for those courses was a natural fit.

Conversely, critical information literacy did not seem to be as natural of a fit for the discourses of other disciplines. Lamont observed that "the 'gulf of mutual incomprehension' that Sir Charles Percy Snow famously posited as separating "scientists" from "literary intellectuals" also separates many social scientists from humanists, as well as many interpretative from more positivist researchers. [S]cholars absorb a variety of beliefs and perceptions about disciplinary cultures, especially each field's approach to producing and evaluating knowledge."[13] While critical theory is seen as a valid theoretical tradition in the humanities and a large section of the social sciences, and in many ways has become integrated into how scholars in those disciplines evaluate scholarship, it has not been accepted into scientific discourse. Lily spoke to the difficulty of working with the sciences:

> I feel like there are departments and disciplines who—like the sciences—that I don't work with very much, who have ideas about how they want their students to understand and

---

13   Michèle Lamont, *How Professors Think: Inside the Curious World of Academic Judgment* (Cambridge, MA: Harvard University Press, 2009), 53.

search for information, and I don't think those ideas have changed very much in the last decade. The scientific process really depends on this structure of... you find information,...problematize it a little bit, gather your own data, then publish it in these places that are respected and get your stamp of approval. So the people who are teaching these new scientists how to think and how to do research have bought into that process. They're not teaching students you should question the very nature of the scientific process.

This can also show up in some of the social sciences where the discipline values positivist types of research. For example, Chris's description of his work with the economics department, where there was a focus on "instrumental sorts of knowledge" is an example of this. He found that in those cases professors were not interested in discussing the more theoretical aspects of information because their disciplinary discourse was too wrapped up in empirical types of knowledge. According to Simmons, scholars working within a discipline come to see their discourse as "natural" and may inadvertently teach students that it is "*the* academic discourse instead of *an* academic discourse."[14] In cases where disciplines seem closed to critical theory, librarians may actually have an opportunity to expand their role in the educational process by serving as "disciplinary discourse mediators." Simmons argues that "by articulating and making visible the epistemological differences in research in the disciplines, librarians can facilitate students' understanding and their scholarly work within a particular discipline."[15]

---

14   Simmons, "Librarians as Disciplinary Discourse Mediators: Using Genre Theory to Move toward Critical Information Literacy," 304.

15   Ibid., 306.

UNDERSTANDING DISCIPLINARY STRUCTURES AS
A PATH TO INSIDER RELATIONSHIPS

In addition to finding ways to be more comfortable with their role and expertise, librarians can work to overcome institutional obstacles by finding practical ways to make their work with information literacy more integral to the educational experiences of students. One way to try to move it from the position of "add-on" to being more a "part of," is by strategizing ways to embed it into specific disciplinary curriculums, including working on institutional-wide committees focused on developing information literacy student competencies, developing strategies for talking with faculty members and academic departments, methodically getting involved at the academic department level to push the information literacy agenda, and working with faculty members one-on-one slowly and patiently to build relationships.

Understanding the structure of academic disciplines can help because the academic activity at colleges and universities is typically organized around and by the disciplines. Reaching a full comprehension of this system can be challenging and takes time, especially because "disciplines are not what philosophers call natural kinds."[16] They emerged with the modern research university between 1870 and 1915, along with almost every aspect of higher education that we are familiar with today.

Modern academic disciplines are "self-governing and largely closed communit[ies] of practitioners who have an almost absolute power to determine the standards for entry, promotion, and dismissal in their fields."[17] Some important features of academic disciplines that impact the professional lives of faculty include largely non-transferable credentials, meaning that their training and education has prepared them for academic work in their specific discipline only; a high degree of specialization is encouraged and often required; and their work is internally regulated so that no one outside the community of experts

---

16   Louis Menand, *The Marketplace of Ideas* (W. W. Norton & Company, 2010), 97.2010

17   Ibid., 105.

of a discipline is qualified to rate the value of the work produced within it.[18]

When we unpack these features, there are some important points that should help librarians feel they have more to offer faculty than they often realize. The degree of specialization and non-transferable credentialing of faculty means they have a strong understanding of their area of study, but they do not typically have a very strong grasp of other disciplines or even other sub-disciplines. As people who tend to feel most comfortable teaching about topics that they know really well, teaching students about the wider universe of information beyond their specialty can be intimidating for faculty. But they are reluctant to relinquish control of their class unless they trust the person they are giving control to. Participants of my study who saw the most success with their critical information literacy classes did two things really well: 1) they built relationships and trust with faculty, and 2) they shared their expertise.

Professors often feel like they are better understood and appreciated by their disciplinary colleagues outside of their institution than by colleagues from other disciplines at their home institutions. "The frequency of interaction across disciplines typically is low, owing to the strong departmental structure of academia, the growing demands on faculty time, and the exigencies of keeping up in one's own field."[19] When librarians take the time to understand the disciplines they support and can talk knowledgably and comfortably about the discipline and how it relates to information literacy, it can go a long way towards helping them gain support for their efforts from the departments they work with. Participants who spoke about being able to have knowledgeable discipline-specific conversations with faculty felt they often had more freedom in what they did with their classes because the faculty trusted them and felt they knew what they were doing.

Developing a strong rapport with faculty members in an academic department and *then* initiating conversations with them

---

18   Menand, *The Marketplace of Ideas.*

19   Lamont, *How Professors Think*, 55.

about how they could more fully integrate critical information literacy into their courses or the entire curriculum of the program was the most common approach of the librarians I interviewed. They hoped that through relationship building and conversations, they would be given more freedom to try new things and be able to develop critical information literacy components.

Developing Critical Librarians

Over half of the librarians I spoke with worked with at least one other person that taught with critical approaches. A portion of those did not think their colleagues would know to call it critical information literacy because they were not familiar with the theory. In his work as an LIS researcher and faculty member, Joe had thought a lot about how critical information literacy practitioners do their work and read widely and talked to many librarians about the topic. He proposed that they "tend to be the one person in their library who is seeing it this way. Or maybe one other person is there with them, too."

Daniel and Hope were the only two participants in my study who worked with more than one other person who used critical methods and content. They were both successful "evangelists," or people who had convinced others in their library to adopt a critical information literacy practice. Both Daniel and Hope had leadership roles around information literacy in their libraries. Hope said that even though she didn't think "they believe in it as passionately or have the same sort of politics that I do about it," she felt supported by her librarian colleagues in her work and appreciated having others to talk to about ideas.

Even having just one other person at their institution who is cognizant of and uses critical information literacy can make a big difference for librarians' comfort level with critical approaches and content. An important aspect of critical pedagogy is nurturing a reflexive practice. Finding others to talk to about ideas, successes, and failures is one of the best strategies teachers can employ to improve their practice. Talking to people who have to deal with the same issues, constraints, and opportunities can help you move to practical solutions for teaching problems more quickly.

Becoming Better Librarian-Teachers

Even though higher education has recognized the importance of continuous professional development and growth to teaching effectiveness for over thirty years, developing librarians' teaching competencies has been mostly left out of that conversation. Teaching and learning centers often call on librarians to provide content on teaching information literacy to faculty, but they are far less likely to allow them to attend as participants.[20] If librarians want to reap the benefits of in-house training programs, they usually have to be created within the library. Many libraries have responded by developing formal instructional improvement programs for their librarians. Other libraries count on the librarians to come up with their own plans for improving their teaching.

Over half of the critical librarians I spoke with shared teaching approaches, ideas, theories, and techniques with colleagues at their institutions in a formal way. For some, this took the form of a teaching group or committee that met regularly to discuss anything related to information literacy, from selecting software for research guides and developing outreach plans to designing instruction sessions and discussing teaching theories. For others, formal communication about information literacy was part of the professional development or staff training that librarians at their institution participated in and may be voluntary or mandatory. For a small number, formal discussions of information literacy happened within larger department meetings or as part of the planning process for first year programs.

Most participants enjoyed informal conversations with colleagues about information literacy in addition to the formal ones. Four participants had only informal conversations with colleagues because of a shortage of time or the lack of a coordinated information literacy program. Those that did not have any type of program in place regretted that the librarians at their institutions did not share pedagogy in formal and planned ways,

---

20   Scott, "Instructional Improvement."

and thought the lack likely stemmed from not having a shared vision for information literacy at their libraries. Andrea "wished... we had a more cohesive vision and more of a collegial approach to teaching," but she thought some of the librarians she worked with had become territorial about their liaison areas in the absence of a formal, structured program. William described a less strained environment with a similar lack of coordination.

While the focus of all of the formal programs was on information literacy in the broadest sense, a few also included some critical information literacy content in their formal discussions. However, most of these did not have it as an integrated concept and tended to have isolated sessions on critical information literacy rather than it being a core component. Hope described the most robust critical information literacy professional development program. She was the instruction coordinator for her library and was responsible for organizing teacher training for the other librarians at her institution. She had woven critical concepts into the overall program and did not treat it as an add-on or special topic. She's "always trying to encourage and promote critical teaching methods," and believes that after six years of doing that, she's "sort of chipped away at the old BI model where you're the sage on the stage and you're just pointing and clicking to a more critical approach."

For most of the librarians, critical information literacy was just a small portion of their formal discussions and it was usually limited to just one or two sessions. All of these sessions were organized and presented by the interviewees themselves, not by others in their institution, regardless of whether or not they were responsible for information literacy professional development at their institution. Michael was in charge of coordinating teacher training for his colleagues. He described a critical session he conducted and explained why doing this type of thing for colleagues can be challenging:

One of the workshops that I organized for my colleagues this past year was on asking questions in instruction sessions. I worked in the kind of questioning that...can raise critical consciousness of various topics and issues that arise within your typical instruction session...to give my faculty colleagues a framework to think about creating learning opportunities that would be more student-centered and that would lead to critical conversations. ... just making that transition from lecturing and demonstrating to having more of a conversation, and constructivist approach to a classroom setting is a very large leap for some of my colleagues.

Anna was not in charge of information literacy training for her library, but she had done a training session for her fellow librarians based on a conference presentation, which led to further opportunities, including an invitation from some of her colleagues to present a session on critical pedagogy. Two participants, Eva and Jack, had created a pedagogy group for their library on their own and invited interested colleagues to join them to read articles, discuss, and practice. Eva described how the group worked:

We worked together to start a pedagogy group that read articles on pedagogy and ... we would discuss it and we had activities that were so much fun. [One activity] the pedagogy group came up with was to list [a bunch of] crazy things and then we put them on slips of paper and then had a workshop for potential teaching. Each group had a slip of paper and they had to come up with something for whatever prop [or prompt] they had. One group got a muffin tin and had to teach a class using this muffin tin. [Another group had to] use a guerilla approach to teaching. [Another] had to teach something by breaking an actual law. So it was a way of kind of opening things up and of twisting things around and it was fun too.

The members of the pedagogy group thought it was very useful and exciting when it was small and voluntary and believed it was the incubator for new ideas, but it did not survive when the members tried to expand it to a larger group because it "lost its exploratory possibilities."

If you are a librarian trying to get started on changing your teaching to a more critical approach, the importance of talking to colleagues cannot be overstated. As the librarians I interviewed demonstrated, librarians sometimes have to initiate the conversation or start the teaching group. A mistake that librarians often make is to think they must be in charge before they can lead the direction of teaching at their institutions. This is wrong-headed for many reasons, but perhaps most importantly, because the people who care the most and are the most informed about information literacy are those who teach it—and those people are the front-line librarians. I have been both an instruction librarian and a manager of instruction librarians, and I was more effective at changing how teaching was done at my institution as a librarian than as a manager. Teachers inspire other teachers and trust other teachers. Don't wait for an administrator to take on the task of teaching improvement. As the following section shows, we need administrators to focus on advocating for and funding information literacy.

Freedom, Funding, and Advocacy: Administrative Support

Librarians do not have high expectations for high-level institutional support for their teaching efforts. My study participants experienced mixed levels of institutional support for their (critical) information literacy efforts, feeling the least supported by college or university administrators and the most supported by library administrators. Table 5 details the direct and indirect support and nonsupport each librarian I interviewed felt they received for information literacy and critical information literacy work from college or university and library administrators.

Participant	LIBRARY SUPPORT				UNIVERSITY / COLLEGE SUPPORT			Institutional IL requirement
	IL	CIL (Direct)	CIL (Indirect)	None	IL	CIL	None	
Hope	X	X			X			GE Outcome
Shari	X	X		X³			X	None
Matthew				X	X	X		GE in progress
Chris	X		X		—ᴬ			GE Goal
Melissa	X	X²	X		—ᴬ			None
Anna	X	X²	X		—			GE Goal
Lily	X		X		X			GE Goal
Jane	X				—			FY Embed
Eva	X		X		—			FY Embed
Joe	X1				—			
Michael					—			None
Chloe	X	X			—			None
Andrea	X				A			GE Goal
Kate	X		X		X			GE Outcome
William					A			None
Henry	X		X		X			GE in progress
Linda	X¹				—			
Jack	X		X		—			FY Embed
Daniel	X	X			X			GE Outcome

¹Current LIS faculty, but were supported when practicing librarians; ²Direct support was from department head; ³She felt supported by her department head, but did not feel like the upper administration supported IL; —not asked about university or college administrative support; ᴬParticipant not asked directly about university or college administrative support, but expressed feelings of ambivalence about support when answering other questions; A-Ambivalent; GE- General Education; FY Embed – Embedded in first year programs/courses

Table 5: Library and University / College Administrative Support for IL and CIL

COLLEGE AND UNIVERSITY SUPPORT

There is a general sense among librarians that upper level college and university administrators do not know a lot, or in some cases anything, about information literacy. Most librarians are so removed from the top administrators at their institutions that support is gauged based on things like sustained financial support, adequate staff, and freedom to chart their own professional course. Even if no one outside of the library seems to know how librarians approach the work of teaching information literacy, demonstrated institutional support for it in general education requirements or in rhetoric coming out of the top offices generally makes librarians feel supported by their college or university administration. For example, Hope felt supported by the administration of her university because they spoke of the importance of information literacy and knew that librarians taught instruction sessions aimed at improving student success, but she didn't "think they know or frankly care about how we go about it."

Librarians that do not feel supported usually feel their library has been financially neglected. Their feelings can be more ambivalent if they have lost trust in administrators who have either previously shown support for information literacy or speak of its importance, but then neglect it when difficult budgetary decisions must be made. William's university went through deep budget cuts and lost half of the librarians and a large portion of the book budget and the library building needed major repairs. The overall budgetary neglect of the library led him to conclude that it was "not really being supported in the way that it's verbally being supported."

A powerful way to build support is to get the library involved in new university initiatives—such as changes in general education requirements, a new first year program, or new or expanded academic programs and majors—by finding ways to insert information literacy in the planning and implementation of those efforts. Kate stressed the importance of involving upper level college administrators, such as the dean of faculty, because they hold sway over the faculty. For example, her college has a senior capstone requirement and she thought this program presented a good opportunity for critical information literacy. She reasoned that if the administration pushed to make information literacy instruction a mandatory component for their capstone, it would be much easier to get faculty support for critical information literacy.

William illustrated how crucial it is to have both faculty and administrative support and buy-in when moving on institutional opportunities. He had successfully organized "an alternative first year program for students entering the university that...[was] based on critical pedagogical theories and was transdisciplinary [and] co-taught." He had approached several faculty members from different departments in the university, with whom he shared common pedagogical interests. The goal for the program was to engage students in "looking at how everything interconnects." He successfully developed the program with the group of professors that he organized and the university approved it for a trial run. Unfortunately, the trial happened while he was on sabbatical in another country and, though the feedback was good and the faculty who taught it enjoyed it, in his absence the administrative support waned. As this case illustrates, administrative support and continuously championing new programs is essential for success.

Uninformed Support: Library Administration and Information Literacy

About three-fourths of those I spoke with felt their library administration supported information literacy directly by providing adequate staffing, funding teaching spaces and professional development, or by administrative involvement in information literacy activities, such as planning, teaching, or promoting information literacy to the wider campus. Librarians who feel supported for their information literacy efforts by library administrators generally translate that goodwill to critical information literacy as well.

Administrators indirectly support information literacy by providing budget for enough staff, an appropriate teaching space, and professional development, but do little to advocate or plan for information literacy in the library or on campus. Most librarians thought a drawback to this type of indirect support was that there was some disconnect in administrators' understanding of how information literacy was or should be accomplished. So while they believed that their deans and directors provided broad-based support for information literacy programs, their lack of knowledge meant they did not know what programs should involve, the amount of work it took to make them effective, or what a successful program may look like.

Joe, a faculty member in an LIS department, thought information literacy was "below the horizon" of many administrators and that they "don't think about this kind of thing very much." He did not think they were against it per se, but rather it was just not on their radar of issues to be concerned with. Linda seconded Joe's feeling that information literacy may not be an issue that occupies them in their daily work, but also thought their level of involvement often depended on the discipline of their academic background before going into administration. She observed that "library administrators have a lot of day-to-day stresses and things that they have to deal with like the roof is leaking." Further, if they did not study a discipline that included critical theory and approaches, administrators are unlikely to have any knowledge of it and are not likely to care if the librarians they manage teach critical or general information literacy.

Occasionally, librarians tasked with instruction work have no support for broader information literacy efforts. Two participants, Shari and Matthew, stated that they did not have support from top library administration for their information literacy efforts. Not surprisingly, librarians are troubled when there is a lack of support from library administrators, and do not see much hope for broadly expanded information literacy programs in those situations.

WHAT CAN ADMINISTRATORS DO?

It should be clear at this point that academic librarians spend an enormous amount of time focusing on building relationships with faculty. While this time seems to be well spent in many ways, it points to two major issues. First, too much of the burden of making information literacy a priority at the institutional level falls to individual librarians, which means that it is likely being accomplished in a hit-or-miss fashion or, in some cases, it ends up being added to university-wide requirements due to accreditation standards without the input of the library or front-line librarians. Second, it often reinforces the power imbalance between librarians and faculty, in which the librarian needs the faculty to use their services for them to be considered successful at their job. Consequently, librarians often feel indebted to any professor who allows them to teach for their classes and are overly careful to make sure they do not upset them in any way by treading too heavily in their territory, making too many suggestions for content, or making suggestions too strongly. Library administrators should lay the groundwork and strive to make information literacy more of a priority at the institutional level, especially if librarians are evaluated based on the number of sessions they teach.

The level of expectation that the participants had for the involvement of the administrators of their libraries in the project of teaching information literacy was disheartening. While most felt supported, their notions of what constituted support was just the provision of basic funding for their positions, classroom space, and time to do their jobs. As one of the most important aspects of academic librarianship in this century,[21] librarians on the front lines should not be the only ones on campus advocating for information literacy. Library administrators should be having those important conversations with other campus administrators to make sure that the significance of it is understood at the highest levels. Administrators know what writing centers and tutoring centers are; they should also know about the same types of support that are offered by the library.

Administrators can draw from higher education organizational theory to develop strategies for institutional buy-in and expansion. Two major theorists that could be especially helpful to library administrators are Birnbaum[22] and Weick.[23] They provided a blueprint for understanding educational institutions as loosely coupled systems, which means that there are many systems (departments, programs, groups) operating within the larger college or university system that are more and less connected and influenced by one another. Weick observed that while organizational theory often asserts that decisions are made rationally, this often does not hold true in practice. In fact, there are many parts of the institution that do not follow rational approaches to organization or decision-making and these parts can

---

21 Ilene F. Rockman, *Integrating Information Literacy into the Higher Education Curriculum: Practical Models for Transformation*, Jossey-Bass Higher and Adult Education Series (San Francisco, CA: Jossey-Bass, 2004).

22 Robert Birnbaum, *How Colleges Work: The Cybernetics of Academic Organization and Leadership* (San Francisco, CA: Jossey-Bass, 1988).

23 K.E. Weick, "Educational Organizations as Loosely Coupled Systems," *Administrative Science Quarterly* 21, no. 1 (1976): 1-19, http://www.education.umd. edu/EDPA/courses/EDPL744-06/2.27.06%20Weick%20Loosely%20Coupled%20 Systems%201976.pdf.

be better comprehended through the lens of loosely coupled systems because they can only be fully understood if they are viewed both independently and as a part of the larger system.[24]

To successfully maneuver within the system, administrators and librarians should think in circles rather than linearly and consider how different groups and subgroups interact with one another and how those interactions change and define the work of each. Different types of institutions have variations in their systems and follow distinctive models of organizational functioning. According to Birnbaum, colleges and universities follow one of the following models: collegial, bureaucratic, political, organized anarchical, or cybernetic. Understanding these organizational types can help librarians and administrators develop strategies for embedding (critical) information literacy in the institution.[25]

---

24   Ibid.

25   For ideas on strategies, see Weiner, "Institutionalizing Information Literacy."

WORKS CITED

Birnbaum, Robert. *How Colleges Work: The Cybernetics of Academic Organization and Leadership*. San Francisco, CA: Jossey-Bass, 1988.

Cox, Bradley E., Kadian L. McIntosh, Robert D. Reason, and Patrick T. Terenzini. "A Culture of Teaching: Policy, Perception, and Practice in Higher Education." *Research in Higher Education* 52, no. 8 (December 2011): 808-29. doi:10.1007/s11162-011-9223-6.

Gorsky, Paul, Avner Caspi, Avishai Antonovsky, Ina Blau, and Asmahan Mansur. "The Relationship between Academic Discipline and Dialogic Behavior in Open University Course Forums." *The International Review of Research in Open and Distance Learning* 11, no. 2 (May 5, 2010): 49-72. http://www.irrodl.org/index.php.

Jaguszewski, Janice, and Karen Williams. "New Roles for New Times: Transforming Liaison Roles in Research Libraries," 2013. http://conservancy.umn.edu/handle/11299/169867.

Jenkins, Alan, and Michael Healey. *Institutional Strategies to Link Teaching and Research*. York, UK: Higher Education Academy, 2005. http://www.vision2020.gu.se/digitalAssets/1345/1345048_institutional_strategies.pdf.

Krishnan, Armin. "What Are Academic Disciplines? Some Observations on the Disciplinarity vs. Interdisciplinarity Debate." NCRM Working Paper Series. University of Southampton National Centre for Research Methods, 2009. http://www.forschungsnetzwerk.at/downloadpub/what_are_academic_disciplines2009.pdf.

Lamont, Michèle. *How Professors Think: Inside the Curious World of Academic Judgment*. Cambridge, MA: Harvard University Press, 2009.

Manuel, Kate, Susan E. Beck, and Molly Molloy. "An Ethnographic Study of Attitudes Influencing Faculty Collaboration in Library Instruction." *Reference Librarian* 43, no. 89-90 (April 27, 2005): 139–61. doi:10.1300/J120v43n89_10.

Menand, Louis. *The Marketplace of Ideas*. W. W. Norton & Company, 2010.

Rockman, Ilene F. *Integrating Information Literacy into the Higher Education Curriculum: Practical Models for Transformation*. Jossey-Bass Higher and Adult Education Series. San Francisco, CA: Jossey-Bass, 2004.

Scott, Walter. "Instructional Improvement: Building Capacity for the Professional Development of Librarians as Teachers." *Reference & User Services Quarterly* 45, no. 3 (Spring 2006): 213-18. http://search.proquest.com/pqcentral/docview/217909102/abstract/BD071D4D0A82466CPQ/1.

Simmons, Michelle Holschuh. "Librarians as Disciplinary Discourse Mediators: Using Genre Theory to Move toward Critical Information Literacy." *portal: Libraries & the Academy* 5, no. 3 (2005): 297-311. http://muse.jhu.edu/journals/portal_libraries_and_the_academy/.

Walter, Scott. "Librarians as Teachers: A Qualitative Inquiry into Professional Identity." *College & Research Libraries* 69, no. 1 (2008): 51-71. http://crl.acrl.org.

Weick, K.E. "Educational Organizations as Loosely Coupled Systems." *Administrative Science Quarterly* 21, no. 1 (1976): 1-19. http://www.education.umd.edu/EDPA/courses/EDPL744-06/2.27.06%20Weick%20Loosely%20Coupled%20Systems%201976.pdf.

Weiner, Sharon A. "Institutionalizing Information Literacy." *The Journal of Academic Librarianship* 38, no. 5 (September 2012): 287-93. doi:10.1016/j.acalib.2012.05.004.

Chapter 7

The Profession: Challenges, Strategies, and Possibilities

When I first started talking to librarians about critical information literacy, it did not occur to me to talk to them about their overall experiences as academic librarians. It seemed beyond the scope of my work of understanding how librarians teach critical information literacy. I should have realized that the yoke of the profession hangs so heavily around most librarians that of course it plays a large role in whether and how librarians are drawn to critical information literacy and in their ability to practice it. After interviewing the first four participants in my study, it became clear that the professional identity and culture of librarians and librarianship heavily impacted how they learned and thought about critical information literacy.

How critical information literacy is received by colleagues at their home institutions and in the profession impacts some librarians' ability to implement it. Librarianship is a profession that highly values collaboration, both in practice and scholarship, so we tend to have a vested interest in working closely with colleagues. When librarians cannot find others at their institution or in the profession to collaborate with on a project—even if that collaboration is simply in the form of discussing certain issues with a likeminded person or presenting their individual work on a joint panel at a conference—it is hard to sustain it. Thus, the place and function of the library profession is important to understanding the state of the field of critical information literacy. In this chapter, I will discuss these professional issues, especially regarding theory in librarianship and information literacy discourse, the practical nature of librarianship, the educational role of librarians, and the role of the *ACRL Standards* in how information literacy is conceived and practiced. The chapter will conclude with some ideas for improving professional and institutional support.

PROFESSIONAL ISSUES: THEORY AND PRACTICE IN LIBRARIANSHIP AND INFORMATION LITERACY DISCOURSE

Many librarians are concerned that there is a lack of theory in librarianship[1] and that librarians do not engage in difficult conversations or allow for robust critiques in the literature or at conferences. When asked about what she thought about the amount of theory in the library profession, Shari responded, "a lot more theory would be amazing. It would be great. I don't know how it would happen, but I think our profession needs a big injection of that somehow." In addition, information literacy discourse does not draw enough on theoretical works and ideas. Chris observed that "one of the things that is frustrating about LIS as a discipline and information literacy discourse is the degree to which people kind of speak past each other in the literature...This happens to a larger degree than in other academic disciplines. When someone comes out with a new writing about critical information literacy in the literature, nobody responds."

Challenging conversations are missing from the disciplinary discourse, in part, because it is a commonly understood professional expectation for librarians to present a positive face to patrons and colleagues, regardless of their actual emotions.[2] Positive feedback and interactions are how academic librarians tend to measure support from those they work with, is a part of the culture of librarianship, and seems to extend into all aspects of the profession. The library conference culture, for example, tends to be pleasant and accepting and does not often include spaces for critical discourse or for people

---

1   Sue Myburgh, *The New Information Professional: How to Thrive in the Information Age Doing What You Love* (Elsevier, 2014).

2   Miriam L. Matteson and Shelly S. Miller, "A Study of Emotional Labor in Librarianship," *Library & Information Science Research* 35, no. 1 (January 2013): 54–62, doi:10.1016/j.lisr.2012.07.005.

to challenge one another's ideas. Anna described the reception of conference presentations as being a "big love fest."

Other participants also spoke about the lack of critical conversations at library conferences, which are heavy on practice and light on theory. Melissa shared a story of how her boss—who she believed was supportive of her interest in critical information literacy—responded to her explanation of a conference proposal that she wanted to submit. After explaining that she was interested in presenting a session on "using cultural studies to improve on information literacy instruction," her supervisor told her that she did not know how that would fit in at a library conference, which are typically focused on sessions that include content such as: "this is an exercise that I did, this is how I taught students how to use the library catalog, or this is how I arranged the settings in our discovery service."

But as one participant countered, it is hard to see how it could really be any other way because "we're a profession of practitioners... [and] when I do [research], I'm hard pressed to know what questions to ask and what to expect and so I think we're just a little bit ill-prepared to have that level of discourse." Still, for academic librarians with additional advanced degrees, it is understandably frustrating to feel like you are part of a "discipline without a discipline," as Eva put it. Andrea's feelings on this are representative of the three participants who earned PhDs and several of those with masters' degrees in other subjects prior to entering the library profession:

> Because I went to library school after doing my PhD I was just sort of stunned that we didn't talk about theory. That was sort of alarming to me. I think I mentioned stumbling upon James Elmborg's article in the first month of...my job as an information literacy librarian and I actually sent him an email saying thank god, thank you for writing this, I really needed to read this because it was really exciting to see someone taking a theoretical approach to librarianship. And a critical literacy approach to boot. So that's actually been something that I've been struggling with.

It is important to note that the scholarly contributions of practitioners in all fields is typically different from that of academics as "practitioners tend to focus on practical, problem-based topics, while academics tend to focus on the theoretical."[3] So it is not surprising that this would hold true for librarians as well. The practical focus of librarians and the literature does not just pertain to the types of articles they write, but also to what they prefer to read. When librarians seek out articles in their field, they are usually looking for articles that can inform their practice and are relevant to their daily work, and they are more likely to write about what they would like to read.[4]

Further, while publishing is a requirement for virtually all LIS professors, a 2010 study found that only 19% of academic librarians "felt they were expected and encouraged to research and publish."[5] This stems from a variety of reasons, with the largest one seeming to be time, in that librarians work 40-hour weeks for twelve months of the year. They do not typically get time off to research and write, so the pieces they publish tend to be shorter and less likely to be based on robust research. As with conference presentations, they tend to be very practical.

A few participants were also concerned that LIS literature in general, and writings on information literacy in particular, were behind the times in terms of how scholars and practitioners are looking at, thinking about, and theorizing their work. Chris argued that the literature "seemed to sort of ignore, or perhaps not engage with a lot of the things that had been written about education in theory or critical social theory and [it did not seem to] be engaged in the key debates in those disciplines that occurred in the past 30 or so years." Eva also found it problematic that the information literacy literature seemed so behind other disciplines. She stated that "stuff about pedagogy and library instruction, they're like 25, 30 years behind and maybe more."

PRACTICAL NATURE OF LIBRARIANSHIP

Most of the participants blamed the practical nature of librarianship as the primary reason for the dearth of theory. Eva observed that "the library community is very pragmatic" and "they might put up with something theoretical" if you present it and tie it in with something

---

3   S. Craig Finlay, et al., "Publish or Practice? An Examination of Librarians' Contributions to Research," *portal: Libraries and the Academy* 13, no. 4 (2013), 404.

4   Finlay, et al., "Publish or Practice?"

5   Ibid.

practical that they can do with it. She talked about a colleague in her library pedagogy group who would say that readings they were discussing in their group were "too philosophical" when they were dense or complex, but certainly not what Eva considered philosophical. This experience, combined with many others like it, led Eva to conclude that there is not "a whole lot of patience...in librarianship" for anything that does not have a clearly practical application.

But Eva, along with several other participants, looked at this practical focus with a certain level of ambivalence. While they thought it would be desirable for more librarians in the profession to be interested in theory and would welcome more theoretically-focused articles and conference papers and presentations, they believed the reality of librarians' daily work *is* very practical in nature, leaves little time for non-practical activities, and does not typically reward people who focus on non-practical issues. Additionally, they expressed personal tensions between the practical demands of their jobs and their interest in critical information literacy.

William related to the ambivalence librarians can feel about their teaching duties. He thought librarians have to be practical because so much of our work, such as developing collections and circulation policies, are practical tasks. But he also thought that,

> it's important that people are beginning to struggle with the theory and actually think about these things. I think it's a really important first step for people to start to think about our practices in the library...why we do them and how we do them and how it [fits] in a larger political and economic environment and that we're not neutral operators. So I think it's important that people start to struggle with those ideas. And I think it does start to affect your practice in subtle ways.

Daniel also described tensions between his interest in critical information literacy and his daily work and the practical expectations librarians have to meet. He has been studying and writing about critical information literacy for around fifteen years and in that time, his career has evolved. He spoke to the practicalities he has had to respond to as an academic librarian and library manager:

Since I [first] wrote on critical pedagogy, I've had to deal with the practicalities...of not having enough staffing, of the shifting information world, of pleasing faculty members—pleasing may not be the best word. But I mean faculty members have a goal and we need to connect with faculty members to be successful....And I've had to learn to fight certain battles and other times recognize that we need to move things forward. Sometimes moving things forward is that just clicking lecture information literacy session and other times it's a more robust conversation about where information comes from. So sometimes the success is just being there with students and not freaking out about a fully realized critical pedagogy model in information literacy.

THE IMPOSSIBILITY OF NEUTRALITY: THE ROLE OF THE TEACHING LIBRARIAN

Despite the challenges that teaching critical information literacy can present, most of the scholars and practitioners I interviewed were positive about their experiences. Following in the spirit of critical pedagogy, they were a highly reflexive group who used all of the information they had to inform their work. They were interested in trying new things and accepted that they would sometimes have failures. They were constantly learning and adjusting their practice, but like many academic librarians, they often felt dissatisfied with their current role in the educational process.

This dynamic seems especially true for reference and instruction librarians who are tasked with teaching students how to use, find, and evaluate information, but are given very little guidance or institutional space in order to do that. Many participants spoke to this lack of space, calling the work they do in information literacy an "add-on" or "adjunct" to the work of the academic disciplines. Some believed that this status—and its accompanying inability to expand beyond traditional hierarchies in academia—was the biggest challenge of academic librarians. It is easy to feel discouraged by working in an environment where your role feels devalued and so completely at the mercy of individual faculty members in the disciplines. Being relegated to this role means that librarians often feel that they are required to hold a place of neutrality and are meant to simply provide the information they are asked for without offering additional context or thoughts about the information or where it comes from.

As educators in their own right, librarians should not pretend to be neutral and they should also not hold to the false notion that libraries are neutral. "A library is inherently selective, as it cannot house all of the documents (or books) available in the world."[6] As selectors for these collections, librarians make choices about what to purchase based on the curriculum and research the library supports and various recommendation sources. Obviously, larger publishers with better marketing and brand name appeal tend to hold more space on library shelves and smaller, niche publishers and alternative presses are less represented. The same holds true for databases, both in terms of which databases are purchased and what the database publishers choose for inclusion in terms of journals, books, and other sources. "Through these processes, librarians tend to select and promote certain kinds of texts, cultural artifacts, and information...[These] selective traditions function as value systems, or sorting and organizing principles, for librarians in various cultures."[7] Librarians, whether they are aware of it or acknowledge it, are by the very nature of their jobs deeply immersed in packaging and presenting, and therefore valuing, certain sociopolitical and cultural norms.

In turn, librarians hold an understanding of information power structures that many faculty members do not have because it is not necessarily part of their disciplinary knowledge. Keeping this knowledge from students is not maintaining neutrality; it is helping to reinforce the status quo. In arguing for using critical literacy theory to teach ESL students, Lesityana states,

> It is not as though we need to agree with any particular position, but rather, working from a privileged institutional space, we need to engage the plurality of discourses not effortlessly but struggling as responsible readers to make sense of and subsequently dispute or reinvent them. This

---

6   H. Inokuchi and Y. Nozaki, "Critical Approach to Asia through Library Collections and Instruction in North America: Selection of Culture and Counter-Hegemonic Library Practices," in *Critical Library Instruction: Theories and Methods*, ed. Maria T. Accardi, Emily Drabinski, and Alana Kumbier (Duluth, MN: Library Juice Press, 2010), 237.

7   Ibid.

is not an argument for a particular ideology. It is rather a depiction of what is fundamental for generating those conditions in which language provides a vehicle for opening up different spaces to allow people to speak to, and be aware of, multiple voices and audiences.[8]

Librarians should approach discussions about information sources in this same way. They do not need to assert their personal opinions on topics, but just acknowledge that there is bias in all sources of information and that authors hold a stance on the topic on which they are writing. In doing so, librarians can teach students that there are conversations about politics, economics, power, and culture happening in the content, context, and structure of scholarly and popular literature, websites, films, and so on, and that part of their job as students is to understand the various points of view in those conversations.

Shari asserted that sharing their opinions about teaching methods and content with faculty is "one of the biggest obstacles for librarians—to think that that's their role [and] to think it's not overstepping their reach." She strongly felt that when librarians present themselves as neutral actors, they remove a lot of their own power and discount their role as educators. "[I]f we were neutral, then we might as well be Google. We've got our own perspectives; we've got to acknowledge that. And that's our job as educators to facilitate this in a way that machines can't," she said. Shari felt that part of the value professional librarians add to education is their understanding of the political and socioeconomic nature of information. Helping students be more critical of information is an important contribution librarians can make. Further, she maintained that when she has held that position with faculty, while it may have sometimes started with awkward conversations, it usually ended with faculty being supportive.

ACRL STANDARDS AND QUANTITATIVE ASSESSMENT CULTURE

Another professional issue that impacted participants' ability to implement critical information literacy at their institutions or to fully

---

8   Pepi Leistyna, *Presence of Mind: Education and the Politics of Deception*, The Edge, Critical Studies in Educational Theory (Boulder, CO: Westview Press, 1999), 132.

adopt a critical approach was the current quantitative assessment and standards-based culture of librarianship. The same assessment culture guiding other parts of education has also taken hold in librarianship. The *ACRL Standards* have guided how academic librarians have conceptualized and operationalized information literacy instruction since their publication in 2000.

As discussed in chapter one, one of the biggest issues presented by the *ACRL Standards* is that they are too general, simplistic, and focused on mechanistic skills. Matthew argued that "the *ACRL Standards* limit our thinking because they treat the whole process as generic." He thought a more effective approach would look at information as contextual with a lot of different elements involved, including disciplinary, professor, and assignment expectations. He contended that "really none of that is detailed [in the *Standards*]. It treats every process as if it were identical."

Some argued that the *ACRL Standards* were out of date and reify a problematic culture of assessment. Michael was respectful of the people who dedicated their professional lives to creating them and thought that "we are better for them having done that." But he still questioned if they are good. He reasoned, "I don't even think standards are good. I think that whole paradigm is, now as we're thinking about it from our current perspective, somewhat problematic—maybe more than somewhat—it's problematic." Shari was "of two minds about the *Standards* in themselves, whether we need standards or that's just setting up this weird sort of very linear system." But she did not use them at all in her teaching because she found them to be outdated and not at all useful for her instructional goals.

The idea that all teaching endeavors should be assessed and that it is not only an expectation, but a necessity, for educators of all stripes, including librarians, has taken hold in academic libraries. Some of the participants mentioned the "Value of Academic Libraries" initiative by ACRL as emblematic of this culture, which is "a multiyear project designed to assist academic librarians in demonstrating library value."[9] This project was initiated by a 2010 report and in the three years since its publication has spurred summits, white papers, grants,

---

9   David Free, "Value of Academic Libraries Summit White Paper," Blog, *ACRL Value of Academic Libraries*, (June 5, 2012), http://www.acrl.ala.org/value/?p=381.

toolkits, and numerous articles and major conference presentations. Joe described this work as being "all business models" and that,

> within librarianship I think there's a tremendous anxiety around proving our value or proving our worth...When I try to talk with people about [the Value of Academic Libraries], there's this big we've got to assess our instruction so that we can prove that we're having an impact...[I]f you go to the English department and you say prove to us that freshman composition is having an impact, what would they say? You can't prove that. We just know intuitively that there is a real need for students to write well and they don't write well but they don't really write well when they are done with the class either. But we still think we need to keep teaching it.

Jane observed that the way initiatives like this are set up, whether you perceive them as good or bad, makes it "very hard not to go professionally where the resources are." She described an experience at the 2013 ACRL conference where she attended a meeting for one of the Value of Academic Libraries' initiatives. During the session, she thought "we need to get in on the cash cow that is assessment in action. We need to develop a plan and put a bunch of stuff in it so we can go on a trip and someone will pay us for it." So while she feels "pretty critical" of it, she finds it "really hard institutionally to not go where the money is and it's certainly things that encourage a mechanistic approach to [information literacy]."

But as Matthew pointed out, even though a robust criticism of assessment culture has emerged that encourages educators to use assessment as a tool in learning and not in such a high stakes way, "administrators like it and unfortunately so do a lot of students and parents and other people involved. And they like things to be neat and tidy and have an easy way to measure success." Chloe asserted that one of the primary reasons that critical information literacy had not taken root in the profession was because it is not possible to demonstrate learning outcomes with it and "we are high-bound to demonstrate learning outcomes, so I don't think its time has come yet."

Conclusion: Creating Space in the Profession for Critical Librarianship

Academic librarianship is both a highly collaborative profession and a largely misunderstood one. Librarians have a professional ethos that includes providing good service, teaching students how to find and use information rather than just providing answers, and "advocat[ing] the ideals that are crucial to the stability of a democratic society and an informed citizenry: freedom of speech, free flow of and access to information, awareness and protection of intellectual property rights, and equitable treatment of those seeking information."[10]

In addition to these ethics, there is an understanding within the profession that librarians will collaborate and be collegial with one another. Participation in professional organizations is a professional expectation that LIS students learn very quickly when they begin their graduate programs. For many academic librarians, involvement in the profession is a necessary requirement for promotion and tenure.[11] Therefore, librarians are often highly affected by the hot topics and trends at conferences and in the library literature both while participating in professional activities and at their home institutions.

While information literacy and some subtopics within it have been considered a hot topic in the library profession for many years, the focus in those arenas tends to be on mechanistic and surface approaches and lacks the critical element that many participants of my study would prefer. Critical information literacy adds a much-needed extra layer to information literacy because it allows for richer and more meaningful conversations with students and faculty about both scholarly and popular information and sources. Librarians who teach with critical methods and content deserve a place at the table so they can share these important understandings with other librarians.

---

10 Kaetrena Davis Kendrick and Echo Leaver, "Impact of the Code of Ethics on Workplace Behavior in Academic Libraries," *Journal of Information Ethics* 20, no. 1 (April 1, 2011): 86, doi:10.3172/JIE.20.1.86.

11 Sue Kamm, "To Join or Not to Join: How Librarians Make Membership Decisions about Their Associations," *Library Trends* 46, no. 2 (1997): 295–306, https://www.ideals.illinois.edu/handle/2142/999.

Updating LIS Graduate Programs with Critical Educational Theories

Eisenhower and Smith argue that pedagogy is "a concept undercultivated in the discourse of librarianship"[12] But "librarians in the academy increasingly see themselves as educators,"[13] which means it is time for librarians and LIS educators to begin to take serious strides towards cultivating both pedagogy and theory in general. Theory is a necessary component of any academic discipline and rigorous critical theory should be a part of the LIS education, especially for aspiring academic librarians, who will work with faculty members and students who are studying various theories. If academic librarians do not have an understanding of at least some major theoretical traditions, it will interfere with their ability to work with and relate to the faculty they are meant to support. Even more importantly, it will limit their ability to critique and fully reflect on the educational process of which they are a part. Eisenhower and Smith sum this up nicely:

> [O]ur library school educations, which feed us techno-managerial speak and quash questions beyond practitioner level, raise broods of liberal faux social-scientists with strident opinions about what users need and how we should serve them, but few thoughts on larger cultural trends that are dismantling our educational systems, such as they are. To be honest, I'm not sure what to do about this.[14]

Develop CIL Curriculum

My study participants struggled with the "how" of teaching critical information literacy. Most developed a strong interest in the topic from personal reading or by bringing ideas they learned from coursework in disciplines outside of librarianship into their library practice. But

---

12 Cathy Eisenhower and Dolsy Smith, "Discipline and Indulgence," in *Writing against the Curriculum: Anti-Disciplinarity in the Writing and Cultural Studies Classroom*, ed. Randi Gray Kristensen and Ryan M Claycomb (Lanham, MD: Lexington, 2010), 127.

13 James Elmborg, "Critical Information Literacy: Implications for Instructional Practice," *Journal of Academic Librarianship* 32, no. 2 (2006), 192.

14 Eisenhower and Smith, "Discipline and Indulgence," 134.

several participants found that even though they were interested in critical information literacy and would like to find ways to integrate it more fully into their teaching, they ran into too many obstacles to be able to make it happen, including a lack of time in the classroom and for class preparation, having to convince faculty that it was a good idea, and simply not figuring out a way to make it work successfully.

Developing an example curriculum could help with all of these. Because it is rooted in critical pedagogy, there is not a "right" way to do critical information literacy, but librarians could help one another tremendously and especially help those who have just discovered the ideas of critical librarianship by developing an example curriculum with teaching plans for general courses and discipline-based courses. These examples could serve to provide a clearer picture of what critical information literacy may look like.

WORKS CITED

Eisenhower, Cathy, and Dolsy Smith. "Discipline and Indulgence." In *Writing against the Curriculum: Anti-Disciplinarity in the Writing and Cultural Studies Classroom*, edited by Randi Gray Kristensen and Ryan M Claycomb. Lanham, MD: Lexington, 2010.

Elmborg, James. "Critical Information Literacy: Implications for Instructional Practice." *Journal of Academic Librarianship* 32, no. 2 (2006): 192-99.

Finlay, S. Craig, Chaoqun Ni, Andrew Tsou, and Cassidy R. Sugimoto. "Publish or Practice? An Examination of Librarians' Contributions to Research." *portal: Libraries and the Academy* 13, no. 4 (2013): 403-21.

Free, David. "Value of Academic Libraries Summit White Paper." Blog. *ACRL Value of Academic Libraries*, June 5, 2012. http://www.acrl.ala.org/value/?p=381.

Inokuchi, H., and Y. Nozaki. "Critical Approach to Asia through Library Collections and Instruction in North America: Selection of Culture and Counter-Hegemonic Library Practices." In *Critical Library Instruction: Theories and Methods*, edited by Maria T. Accardi, Emily Drabinski, and Alana Kumbier, 237-48. Duluth, MN: Library Juice Press, 2010.

Kamm, Sue. "To Join or Not to Join: How Librarians Make Membership Decisions about Their Associations." *Library Trends* 46, no. 2 (1997): 295-306.

Kendrick, Kaetrena Davis, and Echo Leaver. "Impact of the Code of Ethics on Workplace Behavior in Academic Libraries." *Journal of Information Ethics* 20, no. 1 (April 1, 2011): 86-112. doi:10.3172/JIE.20.1.86.

Leistyna, Pepi. *Presence of Mind: Education and the Politics of Deception*. The Edge, Critical Studies in Educational Theory. Boulder, CO: Westview Press, 1999.

Matteson, Miriam L., and Shelly S. Miller. "A Study of Emotional Labor in Librarianship." *Library & Information Science Research* 35, no. 1 (January 2013): 54-62. doi:10.1016/j.lisr.2012.07.005.

Myburgh, Sue. *The New Information Professional: How to Thrive in the Information Age Doing What You Love.* Elsevier, 2014.

CHAPTER 8

CONCLUSION: CONTRIBUTING TO CRITICAL DISCOURSE

In order to fully embrace critical theories in librarianship and information literacy, it is essential that librarians begin to challenge one another and engage in difficult conversations. After having spent a lot of time talking to instruction librarians, it is easy for me to see why we have leaned away from that type of discourse. Our jobs are hard and we never have enough time. We have to deal with faculty, students, and administrators who alternate between not knowing what we do and not respecting what we do. We are a historically feminized and underpaid profession so we want our conferences to be fun and supportive. The list goes on. But to make our work as meaningful as it should be, we have to push harder to make it more critical. An important first step to getting there is to start having difficult conversations as a profession, and then to expand our professional research around critical theory. Librarians have already started these conversations in places like the critlib chats,[1] at special conferences,[2] and in articles, books, and blog posts. This chapter is my contribution to that effort.

---

1   "Twitter Chats | Critlib," accessed March 21, 2016, http://critlib.org/twitter-chats/.

2   "Critical Librarianship and Pedagogy Symposium," *Critical Librarianship and Pedagogy Symposium*, accessed March 21, 2016, http://claps2016.wix.com/home; "Critlib Unconference 2015," accessed March 21, 2016, http://critlib2015.weebly.com/.

(Critical) Information Literacy: A Note on the Distinction and the Theory Base

While my study explored the state of critical information literacy (as opposed to information literacy) in higher education as understood and enacted by academic librarians, there were many points in the findings where it was clear that what was good for one was good for the other, including support from library and college and university administrators, how it was implemented and possibilities for expansion at the institutional level, and working with faculty. But there were also places where the two diverged, including teaching methods and content taught, how the two concepts are understood in the profession, and the types of conversations librarians may have with faculty about information literacy classes or critical information literacy classes.

To clarify the distinction between information literacy and critical information literacy and make clear the instances when the two concepts serve the same purpose, it is helpful to revisit the definitions of each. Librarians have been working on defining and describing research competencies and library research competencies for students since the 1980s and the meaning of information literacy since the 1990s.[3] The debate over the meaning of information literacy is a central topic in librarianship at this point in history. Elmborg argued that "disagreements about what information literacy means are not merely a matter of semantics or technicalities: the lack of clarity has confused the development of a practice that might give shape to librarianship in the academy." Further, "the lack of precision about what information literacy means has prevented critical judgment about its importance."[4] Likewise, there is no clearly agreed upon definition of critical information literacy. Despite the lack of clarity in the LIS literature, I accept Elmborg's assertion that to critically examine (critical) information literacy, clearly articulated definitions

---

3   Robert Farrell, "Reconsidering the Relationship between Generic and Situated IL Approaches: The Dreyfus Model of Skill Acquisition in Formal Information Literacy Learning Environments, Part I," *Library Philosophy and Practice*, November 20, 2012, http://digitalcommons.unl.edu/libphilprac/.

4   James Elmborg, "Critical Information Literacy: Implications for Instructional Practice," *Journal of Academic Librarianship* 32, no. 2 (2006): 192.

are necessary. These definitions guided my study and helped me to organize my thoughts:

Information literacy is "an intellectual framework for recognizing the need for, understanding, finding, evaluating, and using information. These are activities which may be supported in part by fluency with information technology, in part by sound investigative methods, but most importantly through critical discernment and reasoning. Information literacy initiates, sustains, and extends lifelong learning through abilities that may use technologies but are ultimately independent of them."[5]

Critical information literacy is "a library instruction praxis that promotes critical engagement with information sources, considers students collaborators in knowledge production practices (and creators in their own right), recognizes the affective dimensions of research, and (in some cases) has liberatory aims."[6] It looks beyond the strictly functional, competency-based role of information discovery and use and the traditional conceptions of information literacy that focus almost wholly on mainstream sources and views and takes into account the complex power relationships that undergird all of information, including its creation, presentation, storage, retrieval, and accessibility.

Critical information literacy is in a sense an expanded version of information literacy that places the learner at the center in a more empowered role and focuses on the sociopolitical, economic, and cultural aspects of all types and stages of information and the research process. It is very concerned with the power relationships that impact information production and dissemination and tries to move information literacy beyond the purely mechanical and technical. It pulls from critical theories, including critical pedagogy, critical literacy, and others.

Further complications in defining and distinguishing between the two emerge when practice is taken into account. Several of my study participants said that they had librarian colleagues at their

---

5   A. Bundy, ed., *Australian and New Zealand Information Literacy Framework*, 2nd ed. (Adelaide, Australia: Australian and New Zealand Institute for Information Literacy, 2004), 4, http://www.literacyhub.org/documents/InfoLiteracyFramework.pdf.

6   Maria T. Accardi, Emily Drabinski, and Alana Kumbier, eds., *Critical Library Instruction: Theories and Methods* (Duluth, MN: Library Juice Press, 2010): xiii.

institutions that were teaching what they would consider critical information literacy, but their colleagues were not likely to realize or call it that. Critical information literacy as it has been conceived in the literature and in the practice of the participants is steeped in theory. A major reason that many librarians are drawn to the ideas of critical information literacy is because it is theory-based and they yearn for something more in their library practice than they have found with the traditional practice-heavy and theory-light discussions of information literacy. This then begs the question, if librarians are practicing it without knowledge of the theory base behind it, is it still critical information literacy?

Critical information literacy is praxis based, which means that theory and practice are connected and inform one another. As a critical theory, it should include "self conscious critiques" and a "school of thought"[7] so that it is malleable and flexible in response to reflexive critiques and research on practice. Jacobs argued that information literacy practitioners and scholars need to build a theory base that includes critical reflection in order for the work to have meaning for students:

> In terms of information literacy, if we do not use theory as a means toward critical self-reflection and contextualization, our daily practices will come to naught. Similarly, all of our cogent, inspirational theories regarding information literacy will remain "airy nothings" unless we find "a local habitation and a name" in theoretically informed pedagogical practices."[8]

Based on all of this, it would be easy to become dogmatic and declare that all of information literacy should become critical information literacy and all instruction librarians should become theorists. However, a number of the participants of this study thought there was a place for both critical information literacy and information literacy in their work and that it was perfectly acceptable for librarians to not

---

7   H. A. Giroux, "Critical Theory and Educational Practice," in *The Critical Pedagogy Reader*, ed. Antonia Darder, Marta Baltodano, and Rodolfo D. Torres (New York: Routledge Falmer, 2003): 27.

8   Heidi L.M. Jacobs, "Information Literacy and Reflective Pedagogical Praxis," *The Journal of Academic Librarianship* 34, no. 3 (2008): 15.

know the theory if they were not interested. In fact, they thought many of those librarians were very good at their jobs and were good teachers despite their lack of interest in or knowledge of theory. So while they were frustrated with the lack of theory in the profession and, in some cases, with colleagues at their home institutions, as a whole they seemed to think there was a place for both theory-driven and practice-driven librarians.

Most participants believed the nature of teaching people how to do research necessarily includes some mechanical, technical components and that many students who attend college may have little to no experience with using libraries. Starting with the basics is often both necessary and ethically right. However, in terms of their personal professional satisfaction, they wished they had more opportunities to bring critical information literacy into the classroom so they could find better ways to connect the theory with the practice and that there were more opportunities to talk about and engage it with others in the profession.

Problematizing Critical Information Literacy Practice

The question of how to practice critical information literacy is a challenge that will not be easily overcome (and perhaps should not be), as it is rooted in critical pedagogy and "no formula or homogenous representation exists for the universal implementation of any form of critical pedagogy. In fact, it is precisely this distinguishing factor that constitutes its critical nature, and therefore its most emancipatory and democratic function."[9] All but one of the participants in my study spoke of critical pedagogy in terms that reflected a strong Freirian influence, so I used a Freirian lens to analyze the participants' teaching methods and content, to include his "distinctions of monological vs. dialogical pedagogies, his critique of "banking" forms of education as the mere "depositing" of information in the minds of students,

---

9   Antonia Darder, Marta Baltodano, and Rodolfo D. Torres, eds., *The Critical Pedagogy Reader* (New York: Routledge Falmer, 2003): 10.

[and] his conception of *conscientization*,"[10] which I've used to frame the following discussion.

Teaching Approaches: Dialogue and One-Shots

When participants were asked about how they bring critical information literacy into the classroom, one of the most common teaching methods described was the use of critical dialogue. This type of technique is the most common teaching approach employed by critical pedagogues and, along with praxis, is central to the conscientization process. Dialogue can provide a relatively easy entrance point for librarians who are looking to integrate different teaching methods in their classrooms because it can feel fairly low risk and be less intimidating than more complex approaches. Adding space for dialogue is also one of the primary methods for incorporating active learning in teaching, which is a prominent theme in information literacy literature. Most librarians are familiar with the ideas behind active learning and techniques for including it in instruction from reading the library literature and attending conferences. One participant stated that framing the use of dialogue in terms of adding active learning techniques to their instruction could serve as a way to help librarians who are trying to get other librarians they work with to consider trying critical approaches.

While providing entrance points for librarians interested in improving their teaching with the use of critical information literacy is important and dialogue is certainly a good method for doing so, librarians need to be mindful of the purpose of dialogue for critical pedagogy. A challenge that educators face when they attempt to create and facilitate meaningful critical dialogue is having a true understanding of what dialogue means in the context of critical pedagogy and then being able to actually put that into practice. Pepi Leistyana interviewed Paulo Freire about the meaning of dialogue, its role in the conscientization process, and how teachers should approach dialogues with students. Freire stated that "in an attempt to understand the meaning of the dialogical process we have to put aside any possibility of understanding it as pure tactics or strategy...

---

10   N.C. Burbules, "The Limits of Dialogue as a Critical Pedagogy," in *Revolutionary Pedagogies: Cultural Politics, Education, and Discourse of Theory*, ed. Peter Trifonas (New York: Routledge, 2000): 255.

[It] is a way of knowing and not a tactic to involve…[and] requires approaching and examining a certain knowable object."[11]

This means that the dialogue should not be a mere conversation or a device used to involve students at a basic, descriptive level or provide space for them to address the object of study from personal experience alone. While these elements may be part of the dialogue, it should have the larger goal of developing a mutual understanding of something, which includes theorizing it and addressing its larger sociocultural, historical, or political aspects. According to Burbules, "it is widely assumed that the aim of teaching with and through dialogue serves democracy, promotes communication across difference, and enables the active co-construction of new knowledge and understandings."[12] However, using theory to ground the "co-construction of new knowledge and understanding" can be challenging for educators. Leistyna was concerned that progressive educators often neglect theory because they focus too much on the descriptive voice, in which "the authority to speak emanates from the personal—"authentic"—experience in which theoretical explanations of the ideological and sociohistorical formations of such incidents and identities are ignored or simply dismissed."[13]

Neglecting the theoretical and the relational turns the dialogue into nothing more than an inclusionary device or a simple discussion session that only skims the surface of a topic. Some of the participants who used dialogue were aware of the importance of theory in the dialogical process and specifically addressed how they tried to facilitate dialogue that encouraged students to theorize concepts. Further, the concrete nature of the information that librarians typically present may serve as an opportunity in this regard because while it is easy to fall into a simple descriptive discussion about students' experiences and feelings about less concrete topics such as interactions in social situations, their personal reactions to a poem, and the like, it is more difficult to do so in a discussion about something concrete like subject headings and the structure of information. These topics are concrete

---

11   Pepi Leistyna, *Presence of Mind: Education and the Politics of Deception*, The Edge, Critical Studies in Educational Theory (Boulder, CO: Westview Press, 1999), 46.

12   Burbules, "The Limits of Dialogue as a Critical Pedagogy," 251.

13   Leistyna, *Presence of Mind*, 47.

and knowable, while still open to theoretical and philosophical interpretation. Eisenhower and Smith argued that,

> having the advantage of being able to focus on this type of concrete topic is especially fortunate in light of the structure of most library teaching sessions because, while teaching has become central to academic librarianship, the general model remains the "one-shot" session, in which the librarian, ensconced behind a keyboard or in the aura of an LCD projector, expounds to bored students about web pages and databases—an exercise that fails to make an impression, for good or bad, on the research habits of the students. And considering the way many students (and faculty) treat librarians—as service providers of last resort—one has a hard time imagining what pedagogy could apply to this model, unless it were a pedagogy of the drive-in. Inside the aura of the projector, which describes the complete circle of your skill, your aims at least are clear (if their utility is not). Point, click, expound, repeat. Any questions? No? All right, then; goodbye.[14]

Facilitating a meaningful critical dialogue tends to require some level of trust between students and teacher because it requires examinations of personal experiences and the honest sharing of thoughts and opinions. In short, it makes the students and the teacher vulnerable. The single one-shot session is likely to be the only time the librarian and the students in the class interact with each other. There is no time to develop trust or establish a politically and socially equal classroom. In addition, the dynamic for the class has already been established by the professor of the course and if it is one where students are not normally engaged, do not feel comfortable sharing with the other students or the professor, or even has a level of hostility, the librarian will not know that going in, and that can have a debilitating effect on any efforts she may make to engage students in a critical dialogue.

Already, teachers in longer term teaching situations who attempt to enact critical pedagogy are likely to have "unsuccessful moments

---

14 Cathy Eisenhower and Dolsy Smith, "Discipline and Indulgence," in *Writing against the Curriculum: Anti-Disciplinarity in the Writing and Cultural Studies Classroom*, ed. Randi Gray Kristensen and Ryan M Claycomb (Lanham, MD: Lexington, 2010): 127.

in their efforts to find a 'culture of democratic authority' because so often the negotiation and change that are typically a part of critical pedagogy produce results that are hard to predict, plan for, and respond successfully to."[15] Not surprisingly, adding in the problems presented by teaching within the confines of the one-shot model compounds these issues. Participants described at length the problems that came from trying to teach with critical methods, including dialogue, in a one-shot environment. A small number of participants found these problems insurmountable and gave up efforts to try to use critical methods. For others, they were constantly striving with the result of feeling like they experienced some successes and some failures. All of the interviewees were fully aware of the challenges one-shots presented. While they chose to deal with them differently, none of the responses were wrong, but rather reflected how teaching in any form is both complicated and a personal endeavor.

CONSCIENTIZATION, EMPOWERMENT, AND TEACHING GOALS AND ROLES

When participants explained their teaching approaches and content, their instructional goals quickly emerged as a theme. For most, student empowerment was one of their primary goals and the ideal that formed the foundation for their dedication to critical information literacy. This goal has been reflected in other studies of critical educators' identification of critical pedagogy's primary aims and purposes.[16] Liberation and empowerment are central to all of the theories and practices of critical pedagogy and critical theory as a whole. Critical theory's purpose and aims are "not merely descriptive; it is a way to instigate social change by providing knowledge of the forces of social inequality that can, in turn, inform political action

---

15   Alisa Belzer, "Blundering toward Critical Pedagogy: True Tales from the Adult Literacy Classroom," *New Directions for Adult and Continuing Education* 2004, no. 102 (2004): 6, doi:10.1002/ace.133.

16   Mary Breuing, "Problematizing Critical Pedagogy," *The International Journal of Critical Pedagogy* 3, no. 3 (2011), http://www.partnershipsjournal.org/index.php/ijcp/index.

aimed at emancipation (or at least at diminishing domination and inequality)."[17]

While discussing their goals for students, participants often talked about the importance of helping them understand that they should not just mindlessly receive information. Rather, students should be empowered to take part in the scholarly conversation by understanding flows of information so they can see the power relations that undergird all of information (both scholarly and popular). They should also be able to make informed decisions about their own involvement in scholarly conversations. This matches Freire's "conscientization," which is "the process by which students, as empowered subjects, achieve a deepening awareness of the social realities that shape their lives and discover their own capacities to re-create them."[18]

But when talking about their own role in the education process, many of the participants spoke about feeling disempowered. They did not usually use the words "empowerment" or "disempowered" to describe their personal feelings, but they spoke to practical concerns like not having any input into assignments that they were supposed to then prepare students to complete, being unable to get teaching faculty to respond to requests for feedback about instruction sessions, being left out of the curriculum planning process at all levels, and the necessity of prioritizing relationships with faculty over their personal pedagogical goals. Is it possible for librarians to try to help empower students when they are working from such a disempowered place?

Gore and others have challenged the emancipatory and empowerment potential of critical pedagogy and the teacher's role in the process in numerous publications.[19] She argued that "to empower denotes to give authority, to enable, to license," and that

---

17   Fred Leland Rush, *The Cambridge Companion to Critical Theory* (New York: Cambridge University Press, 2004): 9.

18   Darder, Baltodano, and Torres, *The Critical Pedagogy Reader*, 15.

19   Jennifer Gore, *The Struggle for Pedagogies: Critical and Feminist Discourses as Regimes of Truth* (New York: Psychology Press, 1993); Jennifer Gore, "What We Can Do for You! What Can 'We' Do for 'You'? Struggling over Empowerment in Critical and Feminist Pedagogy," in *The Critical Pedagogy Reader*, ed. Antonia Darder, Marta Baltodano, and Rodolfo D. Torres (New York: Routledge Falmer, 2003), 331-48; Carmen Luke and Jennifer Gore, *Feminisms and Critical Pedagogy* (New York: Routledge, 1992).

strong senses of human agency and optimism pervade claims about the teacher as empower-er in ways which portray the teacher's role as crucial and sometimes even omnipotent... The teacher, as the agent of empowerment, is accorded great importance in these discourses. My major concerns are that these claims to empowerment attribute extraordinary abilities to the teacher, and hold a view of agency which risks ignoring the context(s) of teachers' work.[20]

I share Gore's concerns, especially as they relate to the work of academic librarians. While goals of empowerment are admirable and even attainable in some cases, librarians who do not feel a sense of agency may struggle with how to help students feel empowered. hooks offers hope in her description of engaged pedagogy, which she argued "does not seek simply to empower students, ...[but] will also be a place where teachers grow and are empowered by the process."[21] However, she made it clear that in order for that to happen, teachers have to be fully engaged as well because "that empowerment cannot happen if we refuse to be vulnerable while empowering students to take risks."[22]

It is challenging for librarians to let down their guard enough to be fully engaged for a variety of reasons. First and foremost, the students they are teaching are not often "their" class, which can severely limit the possibilities for what they can accomplish. Second, it is standard practice for the course instructor to be in the room with them, often at the librarians' urging. It is difficult to reveal vulnerabilities with students, but it is even more difficult to do so in front of the very person you are trying to impress with your teaching prowess so they will bring their students to you in future semesters. In addition, librarians are currently stuck in an assessment culture, in which they are supposed to constantly prove their worth[23] by making sure they are teaching enough to please their supervisors and assessing

---

20 Gore, "What We Can Do for You! What Can 'We' Do for 'You'? Struggling over Empowerment in Critical and Feminist Pedagogy," 57.

21 bell hooks, *Teaching to Transgress: Education as the Practice of Freedom* (New York: Routledge, 1994), 21.

22 Ibid.

23 David Free, "Value of Academic Libraries Summit White Paper," Blog, *ACRL Value of Academic Libraries*, (June 5, 2012), http://www.acrl.ala.org/value/?p=381.

their instruction sessions in a way that shows their efforts have been worthwhile. This limits many librarians' willingness to take risks with teaching.

In addition to sometimes feeling disempowered personally, some participants questioned whether college students were oppressed and debated if they were in fact the opposite and were poised to become oppressors. A major question that began to emerge for me during data analysis was who gets to decide who is the oppressed and who is the oppressor? And further, where should critical information literacy diverge from the goals and methods of critical pedagogy? Some theorists argue that anyone who has gone through formal schooling has been oppressed and teachers can never be separated from their position of authority and power in any meaningful way.[24] I (and the majority of study participants) tend to take a less severe view and find instead that traditional schooling practices, which includes the way higher education is structured and practiced today, serves to reproduce asymmetrical power relations and class structures. As Dead Prez rapped:

Man that school shit is a joke
The same people who control the school system control
The prison system, and the whole social system...
The schools ain't teachin' us nothing
They ain't teachin' us nothin' but how to be slaves and hardworkers
For white people...
Make they businesses successful while it's exploitin' us
Knowhatimsayin? and they ain't teachin' us nothin' related to
Solvin' our own problems[25]

Some students are oppressed by educational institutions and some are not. This is evident in studies that examine the role of schooling in the reproduction of the class system. For example, Seider interviewed lower income and affluent students at an elite private college and lower

---

24   L. Cooks, "Whose Critical Pedagogy? Communication Education in the Postmodern 'Community'" (annual meeting of the International Communication Association, San Diego, CA, 2003), http://firstnationspedagogy.ca/FNcommunity/sites/default/files/ica03_proceeding_112160.pdf.

25   Dead Prez, "They Schools," n.d., http://www.azlyrics.com/lyrics/deadprez/theyschools.html.

income students at a state university during their first, second, and final years in college to develop an understanding of how class was viewed by students and how it impacted their college experiences and future ambitions. The lower income students had lower aspirations for their futures than the affluent students, even when they attended the same elite college. Those at the state school had the lowest ambitions of all. And none of the students thought class impacted their aspirations or their potential for future success.[26]

Studies like this show that schooling reproduces social class and definitely oppresses some groups, but part of how it reproduces class is by helping to launch those who are already privileged into successful careers, make important connections, and to reinforce the notion that they will have earned their success through hard work and because they were gifted with superior intelligence. Therefore, privileged students attending elite colleges can hardly be considered to be oppressed by higher education. But they can be challenged to confront the institutional inequality that they are a part of and critical information literacy can play a role in that process. Critical information literacy can be a tool used to challenge these structures by providing opportunities for students to see how deeply embedded power relationships are within scholarly enterprises, which encompass the voices they have been told are the ultimate authorities and where they should look for the truth.

It is also important for librarians who are engaging with critical information literacy to be mindful of their own politics and the door that they may be opening when they enter conversations about analyzing power in library instruction sessions. The whole enterprise is full of politics and personal belief. When we discuss critical information literacy ideas with students and try to empower them to understand and engage with information structures more fully, we also introduce the possibility that they may come to conclusions that we do not like.

26   Maynard Seider, "The Dynamics of Social Reproduction: How Class Works at a State College and Elite Private College," *Equity & Excellence in Education* 41, no. 1 (2008): 45-61, doi:10.1080/10665680701774154.

In a fascinating letter to the editor of the *Journal of the American Society for Information Science and Technology (JASIST)*, Buckland[27] disputed claims by Buschman[28] that the purpose of libraries is to forward democracy. Buckland argued for the contextual by saying that "when library systems and resources (or any other technologies) are deployed a socio-technical system is created. The 'socio' component is shaped by the cultural context in which the technology is deployed, so library service would be democratic only accidentally through the happenstance of deployment within a democratic situation."[29] He pointed out that "effective library services are also important for non-democratic political regimes. Lenin and his wife, N. K. Krupskaya, herself a librarian, thought so. Mussolini's Minister of Education was enthusiastic about the role of public libraries in evolving a new Fascist culture, and the Nazis had a vigorous and well-known interest in collection development."[30] Critical information literacy proponents need to stay mindful of these points when talking about empowerment and when considering their project to be a liberal one. As Daniel observed,

> there is a flavor in critical pedagogy that underlies all of it—politicized very radical liberal feel—that I think would rightly turn off some people that may not agree with that political philosophy....I think if you really believe in what some of what critical pedagogy says, you have to recognize that you might be wrong and that there could be a radical conservative critical pedagogy model that could take hold that some of us may not like."

---

27 Michael K. Buckland, "Democratic Theory in Library Information Science," *Journal of the American Society for Information Science and Technology* 59, no. 9 (2008): 1534, http://onlinelibrary.wiley.com/doi/10.1002/asi.20846/full.

28 John Buschman, "Democratic Theory in Library Information Science: Toward an Emendation," *Journal of the American Society for Information Science & Technology* 58, no. 10 (August 2007): 1483-96, doi:10.1002/asi.20634.

29 Buckland, "Democratic Theory in Library Information Science," 1534.

30 Ibid.

RECOMMENDATIONS FOR FUTURE RESEARCH

Critical information literacy is full of possibilities for future research. So little research has been done in this area that the possibilities are essentially limitless. Further research should be done on academic librarians' relationship to critical information literacy and other critical theories, including investigating how librarians developed their interest and how it impacts their careers. A systematic review of what theoretical traditions are taught in LIS programs, including theories and approaches to information literacy, would also be useful. The participants' experiences and perceptions were that information literacy courses are mechanistic in nature. Reviewing these programs would provide insight into whether this is true or perhaps show that LIS programs have evolved since they completed their coursework.

Class observation studies of librarians teaching critical information literacy are the obvious next step after this type of study. While hearing about librarians' experiences and methods was informative, it would provide an important additional layer to observe how critical information literacy practitioners perform in the classroom with students and faculty. In addition, more studies like this one asking librarians to talk about their teaching methods and content and the theory that drives it are sorely needed. A particularly promising approach would be to do a critical information literacy-based study following the methods of Julien and Genuis, who interviewed fifty-six instruction librarians about affective dimensions of teaching library instruction sessions and collected diary entries from fourteen librarians with instruction responsibilities over three months to gather details on how they felt about their teaching.[31] Research connecting theory to practice, or praxis-based pedagogies, in librarianship would help librarians further cultivate their teaching practices.

Further research should also be done on librarian and faculty relationships around critical information literacy. Faculty often express sentiments that library instruction sessions are a waste of time. Investigating whether those perceptions might be changed if the content taught was richer and more critical in nature could provide better insight into what faculty want from information literacy

---

31 Heidi Julien and Shelagh K. Genuis, "Emotional Labour in Librarians' Instructional Work,"*Journal of Documentation* 65, no. 6 (2009): 926-37, doi:10.1108/00220410910998924.

sessions. If the findings were positive, it may help librarians feel more confident about approaching faculty with ideas about teaching critical information literacy. Additionally, as librarians continue to develop strategies and frameworks for talking to faculty about integrating information literacy into the disciplines, it would be helpful to do research into the role critical information literacy could play in those conversations.

More research should also be done regarding the role of various institutional types in teaching critical information literacy. The findings of this study were inconclusive on possible correlations between institutional type and support for (critical) information literacy because there were not enough people in the sample to make sound comparisons. Investigating support for (critical) information literacy programs in relation to institutional type could provide librarians with information to help them prepare for and respond to possible obstacles and opportunities.

Finally, studies taking a broad look at the library profession's receptivity to critical theory would help librarians with an interest in critical information literacy know if they are as alone as they often feel or if there are more opportunities to connect on these topics than the participants realized. A quantitative study to capture data about how many academic librarians have heard of critical information literacy and know about or are interested in critical theory or are open to learning more about it would provide practitioners with a clearer picture of where the profession actually stands on this issue.

WORKS CITED

Accardi, Maria T., Emily Drabinski, and Alana Kumbier, eds. *Critical Library Instruction: Theories and Methods*. Duluth, MN: Library Juice Press, 2010.

Belzer, Alisa. "Blundering toward Critical Pedagogy: True Tales from the Adult Literacy Classroom." *New Directions for Adult and Continuing Education* 2004, no. 102 (2004): 5-13. doi:10.1002/ace.133.

Breuing, Mary. "Problematizing Critical Pedagogy." *The International Journal of Critical Pedagogy* 3, no. 3 (2011). http://www.partnershipsjournal.org/index.php/ijcp/index.

Buckland, Michael K. "Democratic Theory in Library Information Science." *Journal of the American Society for Information Science and Technology* 59, no. 9 (2008): 1534. http://onlinelibrary.wiley.com/doi/10.1002/asi.20846/full.

Bundy, A., ed. *Australian and New Zealand Information Literacy Framework*. 2nd ed. Adelaide, Australia: Australian and New Zealand Institute for Information Literacy, 2004. http://www.literacyhub.org/documents/InfoLiteracyFramework.pdf.

Burbules, N.C. "The Limits of Dialogue as a Critical Pedagogy." In *Revolutionary Pedagogies: Cultural Politics, Education, and Discourse of Theory*, edited by Peter Trifonas, 251-73. New York: Routledge, 2000.

Buschman, John. "Democratic Theory in Library Information Science: Toward an Emendation." *Journal of the American Society for Information Science & Technology* 58, no. 10 (August 2007): 1483-96. doi:10.1002/asi.20634.

Cooks, L. "Whose Critical Pedagogy? Communication Education in the Postmodern 'Community.'" San Diego, CA, 2003. http://firstnationspedagogy.ca/FNcommunity/sites/default/files/ica03_proceeding_112160.pdf.

"Critical Librarianship and Pedagogy Symposium." *Critical Librarianship and Pedagogy Symposium*. Accessed March 21, 2016. http://claps2016.wix.com/home.

"Critlib Unconference 2015." Accessed March 21, 2016. http://critlib2015.weebly.com/.

Darder, Antonia, Marta Baltodano, and Rodolfo D. Torres, eds. *The Critical Pedagogy Reader*. New York: Routledge Falmer, 2003.

Dead Prez. "They Schools," n.d. http://www.azlyrics.com/lyrics/deadprez/theyschools.html.

Eisenhower, Cathy, and Dolsy Smith. "Discipline and Indulgence." In *Writing against the Curriculum: Anti-Disciplinarity in the Writing and Cultural Studies Classroom*, edited by Randi Gray Kristensen and Ryan M Claycomb. Lanham, MD: Lexington, 2010.

Elmborg, James. "Critical Information Literacy: Implications for Instructional Practice." *Journal of Academic Librarianship* 32, no. 2 (2006): 192-99. http://www.journals.elsevier.com/the-journal-of-academic-librarianship/.

Farrell, Robert. "Reconsidering the Relationship between Generic and Situated IL Approaches: The Dreyfus Model of Skill Acquisition in Formal Information Literacy Learning Environments, Part I." *Library Philosophy and Practice*, November 20, 2012. http://digitalcommons.unl.edu/libphilprac/.

Free, David. "Value of Academic Libraries Summit White Paper." Blog. *ACRL Value of Academic Libraries*, June 5, 2012. http://www.acrl.ala.org/value/?p=381.

Giroux, H. A. "Critical Theory and Educational Practice." In *The Critical Pedagogy Reader*, edited by Antonia Darder, Marta Baltodano, and Rodolfo D. Torres, 27-56. New York: Routledge Falmer, 2003.

Gore, Jennifer. *The Struggle for Pedagogies: Critical and Feminist Discourses as Regimes of Truth*. New York: Psychology Press, 1993.

————. "What We Can Do for You! What Can 'We' Do for 'You'? Struggling over Empowerment in Critical and Feminist Pedagogy." In *The Critical Pedagogy Reader*, edited by Antonia Darder, Marta Baltodano, and Rodolfo D. Torres, 331-48. New York: Routledge Falmer, 2003.

hooks, bell. *Teaching to Transgress: Education as the Practice of Freedom.* New York: Routledge, 1994.

Jacobs, Heidi LM. "Information Literacy and Reflective Pedagogical Praxis." *The Journal of Academic Librarianship* 34, no. 3 (2008): 256-62. http://www.journals.elsevier.com/the-journal-of-academic-librarianship/.

Julien, Heidi, and Shelagh K. Genuis. "Emotional Labour in Librarians' Instructional Work." *Journal of Documentation* 65, no. 6 (2009): 926-37. doi:10.1108/00220410910998924.

Leistyna, Pepi. *Presence of Mind: Education and the Politics of Deception.* The Edge, Critical Studies in Educational Theory. Boulder, CO: Westview Press, 1999.

Luke, Carmen, and Jennifer Gore. *Feminisms and Critical Pedagogy.* New York: Routledge, 1992.

Rush, Fred Leland. *The Cambridge Companion to Critical Theory.* New York: Cambridge University Press, 2004.

Seider, Maynard. "The Dynamics of Social Reproduction: How Class Works at a State College and Elite Private College." *Equity & Excellence in Education* 41, no. 1 (2008): 45-61. doi:10.1080/10665680701774154.

"Twitter Chats | Critlib." Accessed March 21, 2016. http://critlib.org/twitter-chats/.

INDEX

CPSIA information can be obtained
at www.ICGtesting.com
Printed in the USA
BVOW04s0139031216

469688BV00007B/88/P